A House Among Vines

Born in 1929, Marguerite Delavenay (now Smith) was taught to speak French at the French Lycée in London before the war, to read, write and love English at Hitchin Grammar School during the war years, after which she took both languages a stage further at Oxford.

She lived on in Oxford to bring up her children, and became a freelance translator under the name of Barnett, being responsible, among other somewhat more literary works, for the English translations of all but the first two of the unquenchable series of historical romances published during the sixties and early seventies, known as the *Angélique* books.

A House
Among Vines

MARGUERITE SMITH

ROBERT HALE · LONDON

© *Marguerite Smith 1996*
First published in Great Britain 1996

Paperback edition 1999

ISBN 0 7090 6473 X

Robert Hale Limited
Clerkenwell House
Clerkenwell Green
London EC1R 0HT

2 4 6 8 10 9 7 5 3

Typeset by
Derek Doyle and Associates, Mold, Flintshire.
Printed in Great Britain by
St Edmundsbury Press Limited, Bury St Edmunds, Suffolk.
Bound by
WBC Book Manufacturers Limited, Bridgend

Contents

Acknowledgements

My warmest thanks go to Gordon my husband, to Faith Evans, to my children, my friends, and my congenial computer, for their unfailing patience, encouragement and support.

History is the recital of facts represented as true.
Fable, on the other hand, is the recital of facts represented as fiction.

Voltaire, 1764. *Philosophical Dictionary*

I The Midday Plane

As I sat looking idly out over the port wing at a sea of dazzling cotton-wool clouds, I suppose I must have dozed off for a few minutes. For suddenly the clouds were gone, and I could see the coloured map of France lying way, way below. Then I glimpsed my old friends the Dordogne and the Garonne at the point at which they flow into one another, a bit upstream from Blaye, there to be re-christened the Gironde, yet swirl on for many a mile, still clinging to their old identity, brown and grey parallel ribbons of water, flowing side by side in the wide bed they have carved together through the green, grey and yellow patchwork of tiny fields. We were beginning our descent to Bordeaux.

The midday plane on that early June day was bursting with holiday-makers on their way to the South-West of France, and I was suddenly aware that my darker, weather-beaten face must have marked me out as a passenger returning home rather than setting off for a foreign land. For France was indeed my home: enchanting, exasperating France, so familiar now, yet so utterly different from the England I had grown up in.

For the first time ever, I had actually enjoyed London – every minute of the three exhilarating days I had just spent there. Of course, the sun had shone unabated on the picnic on Primrose Hill, on my hastily snatched shopping expedition, and above all on the wedding. And what a wedding! But three days had been enough, and the sight of the car I had left at Mérignac airport filled me with eager anticipation of the quiet joys of home.

The sun shone over Aquitaine too, but then that was not uncommon at this time of the year. The house, splendid in its isolation, welcomed me into its cool, peaceful haven. Tomorrow I must shop for food and cut the grass. Meanwhile, after unpacking my things and putting away my suitcase, I did a tour of the garden, a bit of watering, an hour or so's reading, followed by poached eggs for supper and an early bed.

But sleep eluded me that night. I who could sleep dreamless through the hammering of winter gales against the bedroom shutters and the deafening bombardment of summer thunderstorms around my hilltop house, I who had but to lay my head on the pillow and wake up to find the sun about to rise, that night I could not sleep. My head swam with images. Memories that had lain dormant for up to twenty years danced tirelessly before my eyes, begging to be given back the flesh and blood that had once been theirs.

The wedding had been full of friends. Almost every place-card at the luncheon bore the name of someone I knew, even though their faces were less familiar to me than the books they had written. In a sense I was the odd man out in this distinguished company: just a relative, not a writer.

But the fact that I lived permanently in France seemed to interest my table companions, curious to know more about what it was really like to have settled here. They, of course, had all travelled widely, knew France well and loved it. At least they did not, as many people so unfortunately do nowadays, think of the South West as a vague extension of Provence, a name that seems to be on everyone's lips, even though the images it conjures up are for the most part sadly superficial.

My table companions had an excellent literary knowledge of France, and knew everything there was to know about all the places marked '*Vaut le détour*', whether for their historical, architectural or gastronomic interest. Gault Millau was their Bible, and their enthusiastic talk about wines left me quite out of my depth.

But what they did not, and could not, know was what it felt like to have lived for twenty years among the French, the rural, rustic French, the French peasantry of the seventies and eighties, the French who regard anyone living north of the Loire as '*Un cochon de Parisien*', the French who pronounce every mute 'e', thus making themselves incomprehensible to their northern brethren to the point of having to call in interpreters – French-speaking resident English, more often than not – to enable them to understand one another!

I was once in the company of a native-born Frenchman of considerable education and distinction who, faced with one of my rural neighbours, had to ask me discreetly (in English) to 'translate' what the farmer was saying to him, so totally incomprehensible did he find his speech. I, who lived in daily contact with this accent – and I don't mean the Gascon patois, which I don't claim to understand – found it easier, even if not always immediately intelligible in every speaker's mouth.

In this area, the English are made welcome: 'Just another invasion.... We are used to it by now!' the local people will tell you, while the French from other parts of France are known to them as *'des étrangers'* – foreigners. It's only partly a question of language. It is not easy to be really accepted here, but the English who speak some French, or who at least make the effort to do so, are better liked than the Parisians or even, surprisingly, than people from Bordeaux. You really have to be born here, and have lived in the same village all your life, before you can claim to belong.

Now my table companions had never eaten in genuine peasant homes, only in restaurants, or the homes of expatriate friends. They had never been called upon to drive a tractor under a blazing July sun, to attend the slaughter of the pig destined for the freezer, to help a neighbour deliver a calf. Their comfortable lives in NW1 allowed them regular pilgrimages to some beloved part of France, during which they would indeed meet and converse superficially with the French in their hotels, their campsites, their shops. But *my* life was not like that: I simply couldn't begin to tell them what it was really like, and I feared they would not understand what I was trying to convey.

An old college friend, born and bred in London, once said that she could not imagine how I could bear to live as I did, cut off from the theatre, from concerts, from 'stimulating conversation'. But then London is her village; mine is different. And I love it in spite of these shortcomings.

As I lay there in the soft, silent darkness of my home, I thought of those twenty years, spent for the most part alone in my big, rambling house in the middle of nowhere. Although I eventually made acquaintance with some of the English and Dutch settlers, my life centred largely around my immediate neighbours. I used to be co-opted to plant tomatoes, potatoes, to gather up plums for prune-making, to pick strawberries, and the tomatoes I had helped to plant. I had done many a *vendange* with the rain pouring down the back of my neck, and some when my face and hands were blackened by the sun as much as by the grapes. I had learned how to grow my own vegetables, to keep hens, bantams and ducks, even a sheep, and to breed rabbits. I bottled fruit from the orchard and made jam. One chilly February day, after the horrific ceremonial slaughter of the pig in which I had a half share, I dissected my portion on my kitchen table, alone with a cleaver in one hand and John Seymour's *Complete Book of Self-Sufficiency* in the other, then prepared the joints for the freezer, made and sterilized jars of pâté. It was not always an easy life, but a busy and very satisfying one.

I was once summoned at two o'clock in the morning by a neighbour thumping on my bedroom shutters, calling out that they needed 'two men and one person' to help the vet deliver a calf by Caesarean section. Hastily pulling on an old track suit, I was ready to assume either role, and ended up passing the vet's instruments to him as he asked for them one by one, while I watched, fascinated, as he anaesthetized the cow's nether quarters with an epidural injection, cut through seemingly endless leathery layers of her underparts and, with a second pair of strong hands to help, gently lifted out a large, handsome male calf. I wouldn't for all the world have missed seeing that lusty baby bull totter over to his mother to be licked dry as she rose to her feet after the last stitch was tied.

But I could hardly tell them all this at the wedding luncheon: the canvas was too vast, too much had happened over those years to be compressed into a few inadequate phrases. And yet, how could I ever hope to record what I had experienced and witnessed of life down here, unless I sat down and wrote about it? It suddenly became a matter of urgency. I had no idea how to tackle the task I set myself, but was determined to try. If others had found the trick of it, perhaps I too could find a way to bring new life to my memories, so that others might enjoy them too.

II My Bolthole

It was almost by accident that I came to live on my own in France, for the house was there, still pretty basic but beautiful, when my marriage broke up, and it became my bolthole. The original intention had been to retire there as a couple, like so many other British settlers hereabouts, and meanwhile it had been used as a 'holiday home'. More time had been spent working on the house during university vacations than getting to know our neighbours, so when I finally opted to live there alone, after nearly thirty years of married life, I cannot say that I had anything beyond a pretty superficial knowledge of the environment I was coming to.

Yes, there was 'our' French family, the farmer we had bought the house from in 1972: Gaston, his wife Eliane and their children. They lived a good four kilometres away by road, although their house was just visible from mine across the intervening valley, through which ran a small stream, inhabited by a myriad of frogs that would set up a night-long almost deafening chorus whenever the wind swung round to the west, forecasting rain. With frogs like that you didn't need the weather man on the radio.

Gaston and his family had always been most hospitable and friendly, insisting that we come over for a meal whenever we arrived on holiday. We amused them, partly because we brought a breath of fresh air from a world unknown to them, but especially because that breath of fresh air came in French, which greatly simplified our relations and made true communication possible.

They had eyes like hawks, useful for keeping watch on our house in our absence, but it also meant that they always saw us arrive, and were mortified if we did not go over and greet them then and there. They had absolutely no concept of what a strain it was to drive from Le Havre or Calais in a day, often towing a trailer full of furniture, and arrive to find a dirty house, damp beds, and everything waiting to be done. All one wanted to do was unpack, unwind and tumble into bed. The furthest Gaston and Eliane had ever been was Bordeaux: their life was so totally different from the one I knew at that time, that no amount of explaining cut any ice with them. So visit them we must.

Not that we did not have lots of fun with them. They had a lively if somewhat basic sense of humour and were helpful and kind, Gaston in particular. Eliane was a trifle more wary of us, and did not join as enthusiastically as he did in the elaborate jokes her husband used to set up to amuse us, though I have to admit that some of them I didn't find terribly funny either.

One of the best was when Gaston acquired, by mail order, from Holland, I think, a rather revolting inflatable doll, with bright pink cheeks and silky black hair, as straight and shiny as anything the Far East could produce. This creature he dressed in skirt, blouse and cardigan, and placed in one of the rear seats of his car, so that she looked, from behind the car, even from close to, just as if she were the friend they said they had brought round to meet me. I was told that their 'cousin' was very shy, and needed to be encouraged to get out of the car and come into the house. Of course I went out to the car immediately, saying all the things they had hoped I would – '*Mais Mademoiselle, ne restez pas dans la voiture ...*' – until, to their great delight, I found myself face to face with those highly coloured rubbery cheek bones, those long black lashes and blank, staring eyes.

But when I eventually came to settle permanently, some three years later, Gaston, and particularly Eliane, were mystified, and I was to find my relationship with them subtly altered as the years went by. I did not choose at first to be too specific about the break-up, but told them that I was there alone 'for the time being'. It was some time after that I learned that I was referred to in the village as '*La Divorcée*'. And although I had not in fact divorced, I found that my status changed in an indefinable way: Eliane, for instance, though remaining friendly enough, clearly was not going to have Gaston spending any more time than absolutely necessary near my house, now that I was there alone. Perhaps she knew that any woman living on her own, even if not in her first youth, would inevitably fall victim to local male concupiscence, and she was going to take no chances.

Now the house had been theirs from the time they had bought the land from the Jeanblanc family, who had been in it since the early twenties, and since Gaston's fields ran right across the valley from their farm to the back of my house, he had of course to plough and harrow, then sow and harvest whatever crop he planted on them each year. I noticed that Eliane always found some outside task to do when he was working near my place, as if wanting to keep an eye on him, although I had never given her the slightest cause for thinking this might be necessary. Perhaps she knew her husband, and did not want to tempt providence. So our relationship became slightly more strained, more day-to-day, lacking the 'events' our arrivals and departures had previously constituted, and such contact as my lack of transport allowed, became more routine and mundane.

There was also an element of jealousy. For initially we had been 'their' family – '*nos Anglais*' – and for three years had made ourselves available to them, and only to them, since we knew no one else. But once I had settled permanently on my own, I began to meet other neighbours, and my contacts with some of these clearly did not meet with Gaston and Eliane's approval. They would never tell me why: the matter was never in fact discussed, but if ever I mentioned certain families, they would sniff and say: '*Ils ne sont pas intéressants, ceux-là*'. Which, in their way of saying things, could have meant anything from 'they are a lot of bandits and we don't speak to them' to a mere 'we think they are not people you are likely to get on with'. There are, I found, so many unspoken taboos, so many simmering antagonisms in the life of a village and Commune like ours, that I felt I must opt for making friends where I thought fit, which of course changed things where

Gaston and Eliane were concerned.

After a few weeks I simply *had* to buy an old moped, and when I eventually managed to obtain a very cheap, small car – an ancient Renault 4 (known among the English as a 'Noddy car') – I remember asking Eliane how far it was to some town I had not yet managed to reach. Her reply was startling, to one coming from a busy city. 'It all depends on how many people you meet on the way,' she said, with a perfectly serious face. I took her point: she, like everyone else around here at that time, who bumbled around in very elderly vehicles, often diesel Mercedes approaching the end of their long lives, would never think of not stopping on the road to chat with every neighbour or acquaintance she happened to pass. On the side roads everyone knew everyone else, which might explain why even to this day no farmers round here ever use their direction indicators. 'Everyone knows where I live', they tell themselves, as they swing suddenly to the left across the road in front of you and vanish down a track you did not even know existed.

I soon realized that living alone here, and all the year round too, was a very different matter from just holiday-making *en famille*. It was hard having no transport at first and almost no money, beyond the stingy proceeds of the last translation I had done in England, before packing my bags for France. Translating is one of the worst paid jobs in the literary world: I suppose that is one of the reasons it so often seems to be badly done. And in the business world, people regularly seem to think that all you need is 'someone' on the staff 'who knows a bit of French/German/English or Japanese' for them to be able – at little or no cost to the firm – to translate the instructions/guide books/what-have-you. We are all too familiar with the results.

So economy had to be the strict order of the day. I remembered some of the things my mother and sister and I had done during the war: every bit of string laboriously unknotted and tied in a neat bundle, then stored in a shoe-box; every newspaper and piece of wrapping paper carefully folded for future use; every candle-end kept to make new candles. Boxes were always stored: I still find it almost impossible to part with some of the glorious cartons things come in nowadays, and my barn is always stacked with boxes of all shapes and sizes that 'might come in handy one day'.

I dug a vegetable patch and grew most of what I needed, or

rather I ate only what I could grow, which was not quite the same thing. And neighbours were always generous with their surplus fruit and vegetables. I did eventually buy a freezer, since it avoided much waste, when there was a glut of fruit, for instance, or simply not time to deal with it all at once.

Anyway, when I came to live here there were a few hundred pounds in my post office savings book, which in due course I transferred to the *Livret 'A'* in my local *poste*, and I brought myself, and what I could carry of my possessions, to my nearest railway station, being obliged, of course, on that unique occasion, to finish the journey by taxi.

It was a warm March day, and the sun made up for the other deficiencies of my life. I had no bathroom, only a kitchen sink with, I am glad to say, at least cold running water. I would have to install one of those small gas water-heaters over the sink before the winter. But there was adequate furniture: a large and a small table in the kitchen, six chairs, a huge old French *armoire* that held all my kitchen supplies, a fridge, and a short kitchen worksurface on either side of a cooker, with cupboards below for china and glass.

In the one large bedroom was a chest of drawers with a small Victorian tilt mirror on top, a wicker chair, another French *armoire* arranged as a hanging cupboard, and one of the local beds, known as a *lit de coin*, with a high, solid wooden head and foot, carved, like the strip that ran along the bed base, on one side of the bed only, the intention being that it should be placed lengthwise against the wall, rather than standing out into the room. And since these beds have wheels built into the underside of the frame, wheels that turn in only one plane, enabling you to pull the bed out from the wall and push it in again, but making it impossible to move it in any other direction, one had, because of its weight, to bow to tradition and place it along the wall, or be unable to shift it. It was meant for two people. Being only 1.20m-wide – about 4 foot – it made a very comfortable bed for one. Two had to be very close in every way to be able to sleep well in it. And it was so short that anyone over five foot seven was obliged to stretch out diagonally or hang their feet over the edge.

In the middle room of the house was the main fireplace, complete with pothook over the fire. A large table stood under the window, a corner cupboard in one angle, and a couple of settees – one of them a put-you-up – stood on either side of the fire. I really had all I needed: the frills could be added gradually. And there was the huge, dark barn to 'colonize', with its old cow stalls, its beaten earth floor and its slightly spooky feel. I was glad that the door from the end of the central *couloir* had been replaced, and had at least a lock of sorts, with a key, since at that stage the entire barn, which was in three distinct sections, was still open at each end, and along the back, not only to the elements, but to anyone who might have chosen to wander round the house by day or by night.

I soon learned, however, that most of the people I got to know locally were strangely frightened of the dark, and barricaded themselves into their homes once the sun had gone down. They regarded me as a curious, foolhardy oddity, living alone so far away from anyone else. And yet for me this was the greatest charm of my old house. I did not even have a telephone, and was told that it might take several years before I got one.

The house itself was square, measuring twenty metres in each direction, with a gently sloping roof that rose up to its ridge over the front third of the house – the part that held the living accommodation and had a loft you could stand up in above it – then went on down over the much larger barn area to reach a point on the west side that just allowed a low door to open beneath. The ends – you can hardly call them gable ends, because they were not vertical – were tiled with flat tiles and described an elegant, long, softly curving triangle, which the local builders called *une Pente Brézilienne* (a Brazilian 'slope'). These are becoming a rarity now, since the special flat tiles used for them are no longer made.

The original house had clearly consisted of only two large rooms and the central wide *couloir* (with, of course, some of the present barn behind). The first room (with its secondary chimney), which I had made my kitchen-dining room, showed signs of having been added at a later date, though what that date was I have never been able to establish. It would seem that there had been several houses scattered around the site since at least the fifteenth century, but now only mine remained and I think thát even if the first four feet or so (noticeably thicker than the walls above that level) date from earlier, the rest had been rebuilt perhaps many times over the years. The pattern is so classic, so typical of this area, that it would be very hard to put an accurate date to it.

It was built, like most of the local houses, of random pieces of hard, creamy-white stone, carefully positioned in order to interlock perfectly. The walls were double-skinned, the space between the two being filled with earth, and a very minimum of weak mortar used on the outside to hold all the stones together. I well remember the terrible discovery I made of this space: I was installing a new ceiling over one room, and had stripped off the 'floor' of the loft above. As I moved carefully about the exposed beams to remove all the nails from their upper surface before proceeding further, I found myself looking down onto the top of the inside walls of the house that did not continue into the loft above. Finding them full of mouse droppings, scraps of paper and gnawed maize haulms, I eased myself gently down the ladder and went in search of the vacuum cleaner.

But when I began to suck out the filth of ages, I suddenly realised that it *was* the wall, at any rate the centre of it, and that this was what was supporting the two outer skins of stone! By this stage there was nothing for it but to mix several trugs full of strong mortar and pour it into the gaping hole I had so rashly created, hoping that the house would forgive me this wanton and thoughtless attack on its age-old integrity.

III   The Jeanblancs
(a bit of history)

'La maison Jeanblanc' was not the real name of my house, not the one you would find on a detailed map, but it was the one used by all the local people, who refer amongst themselves to most of the houses by the names of those who lived in them. Very often the same family has owned the same land and lived in the same house for generations, since their land represents their entire wealth and their means of subsistence.

The Jeanblancs had come to this region from Brittany during the mid-twenties, when land and houses were offered free to 'immigrants', in particular from Northern Italy and from the Brittany peninsula. Their only obligation was to cultivate the land in an area that had become seriously depopulated. Not that there were no Gascons left, they had not deserted the country, but they seemed to be unusually infertile, producing, more often than not, merely one child per family. And of course the 1914–18 war had brought death to countless men and boys, leaving widows alone on the land with no one to help them. It was no wonder that farms were abandoned and farmhouses, in due course, overrun with weeds. It had taken five days for the Jeanblancs to hack their way through the brambles to the door of their new home.

That house had seen the birth of eleven Jeanblanc children: the local doctor, who had just retired when I came to live there, told me that in those days it was inaccessible by car, and that he had been obliged to leave his vehicle at the bottom of the hill at the far end of the house, and, carrying his Gladstone bag full of the instruments and other equipment he thought he might need, clamber up through the vines to attend most of these births. Madame Jeanblanc had been, from the time he first knew her, a confirmed alcoholic, incapable of cooking or keeping the house even superficially clean, while the 'old man', who also drank to excess on occasion, was despotic and violent, greeting any unexpected caller with a loaded shotgun, which he refused to put down until he had finally decided that the intruder presented no threat.

How they managed to accommodate eleven children and four adults in what was basically a three-roomed house, I found hard to imagine. I could see that the grandparents must have lived independently at one time in the end room, for the original fireplace had been blocked off and a stove pipe thrust through the side of the chimney flue, no doubt for a wood-burning cooker, while in the far corner of the room a pull switch – that must once have turned off the central light – remained on the wall above a large rectangle of relatively clean and unworn floor tiles, over which their bed had clearly stood.

In the middle room the same kind of cooker had also been installed, but the open fire kept alight at the same time, which explained the smoke-blackened beams, since you cannot get a chimney with a hole in one side to draw properly! The hearth was so wide that a two metre log would lie straight across it, which saved a lot of cutting, although burning wood like that positively gobbles it up. A metal bar ran across the back of the fireplace, about three feet from the ground, with a solid black pot-hook hanging from it. This had been the main family room, *la cuisine*, as it was always called, where they all ate and the parents slept, so I was told, on old blankets beside the fire.

After the middle room came a wide passage, known as *le couloir* – the corridor – with a door at the back into the barn, and one at the front into the garden. It seems to be a common design around here, among the rather 'grander' houses. The ancient stone sink was built into the front wall, and water fetched in a bucket from the well opposite the door, after which it was emptied down a short length of pipe that ran through the wall, or flung straight out through the door onto the garden. When the wind blew cold from the east, that pipe funnelled it into the house most effectively. This sink was all they had: it had been in daily use for washing up and family ablutions, such as they were, until the house was abandoned a few years before I bought it.

The last room, to the right of the doorway, had been divided into two roughly triangular rooms, each with a window, one to the east and one to the north, and the inevitable central door, like all the other rooms, so you could see from one end of the house to the other. When I asked one of the Jeanblanc 'boys', who was at that time nearly seventy, which of the two rooms had been the boys' and which the girls', his reply came with a chuckle: 'Good heavens, there was no such organisation in our house! You just got into a bed where there was still a space, and considered yourself lucky at that!'

So you see, the house was full of ghosts. They did not trouble me, however, since they all seemed to be friendly ghosts, and we lived in harmony together. They forgave me for demolishing the diagonal wall across the 'bedroom', thus returning that part of the house to its more elegant proportions. They also forgave me for removing the solid wooden outside doors to the far end room and the *couloir* – doors of which the bottom twelve inches of timber had, in any case, rotted away completely – and replacing them with twelve-paned three-quarter-glazed doors and shutters to match those I had replaced on the existing windows.

Whether the ghosts forgave me the luxury of a loo and a comfortable bathroom, I could never be quite sure, for I always found that part of the house slightly spooky. But the Jeanblanc 'boys' – two of them with their wives – were full of enthusiasm for everything I did to 'their' house, and would ask one another why *they* had never thought of doing some of these things, like painting the walls white, as I had done. And to tell the truth, I was more than thankful that they had not, or I might have had to strip coats of paint from the panelling, or worse, from the stone fireplaces, which, happily, had never been touched.

For many years the four of them would visit me at cherry time, and go away, of course, with a large basket of cherries. For they, as boys, back in 1928, had grafted the three cherry trees that now dominated the orchard and gave liberally of their sweet fruit every summer. I have never encountered, before or since, such exquisite cherries.

They had held their wedding celebrations in the barn, no doubt with the twelve cows shuffling uneasily in their stalls along one side, as they tugged at their hay then chewed the cud, while the feasting and dancing went on into the small hours on the beaten earth floor directly behind the house. They had moved the last of the hay into another corner, beyond the cows, to make way for the party: the weddings had been planned for just after Easter before haymaking began, after which the huge barn would be gradually filled again to the rafters with hay and straw. Music for dancing on such occasions, they explained, was invariably provided by a young fiddler from the village, more enthusiastic than accurate, but always welcome, since he never put down his fiddle until the last of the guests had departed. He was, incidentally, the chemist's assistant during the daytime, and managed somehow to qualify as a chemist himself over the years, the 'boys' told me.

Then their mother died, poisoned by alcohol, and their father eventually went off his head and was taken away to an institution, and the whole place became unmanageable. One of their brothers lived on there with his wife for a while, they said. He found a job that he could cope with, about twenty kilometres away, and would cycle there daily. He wasn't very bright, in fact, and not many people wanted to employ him; and he couldn't manage the farm, so the land was rented out, and each of the children received a tiny income from the proceeds.

Now, this brother, being simple, used to be teased a lot, and one day someone told him that his wife 'entertained' while he was away at work. This sent him into a frenzy and, instead of taking his lunch to work, he began to insist on cycling home for lunch each day, and back again to work, which of course left him utterly exhausted. His wife, who kept the house clean, tended the vegetable garden, looked after the hens and cooked, washed and mended for them both in his absence, knew nothing of these tales, nor did she understand her husband's insistence on riding home to lunch. Unfortunately, his jealousy got worse and worse, no doubt stirred up by people who thought it funny, until one day when, unable to bear the pain his own imagination was causing him, he shot his wife and hanged himself. A sad story, the old men added, with a far-away look in their eyes.

After that they all agreed to sell the place to Gaston, who, after some years, decided to part with the house and a single acre of land round it, to pay off some of his debts. That was when I bought it.

IV Monsieur Pochon's Emporium

I suppose one of the first people I got to know in the village itself was the man who owned the general store on the main road opposite the church.

Our village, like my house, was built on the top of a small hill, and was roughly circular, following the contours of the land. Unlike many of the villages around here, it had never been razed or burned down, but had survived from the early part of the fourteenth century. Epidemics it had known, but these had touched the inhabitants rather than the fabric of the village. The eighteenth, nineteenth and, above all, twentieth centuries had left their mark, however, and not always for the better, I fear.

Although small, it had amenities that were by no means always available in many a larger agglomeration: we had a church of some distinction, two general stores, a school that went from nursery classes for the two- to five-year-olds to the eleven- to twelve-year-olds being prepared for the middle school in the nearest town. There was a café, run by cheerful, pretty Henriette and her friendly old soak of a husband, and a bar where meals were served by red-headed Fanny whose husband Marcel made an excellent red wine and looked after the customers, while she prepared succulent dishes in her kitchen behind the bar. We had a flourishing post office, a chemist and a doctor. We lacked a bakery, but both the general stores and 'Chez Fanny' sold bread, which was delivered fresh to them daily, like all self-respecting French bread. On the outskirts of the village there was an excellent carpenter and, beside his workshop lived a plumber-electrician.

The heart of the village consisted of the *Halle*, a covered market square, where once a week the shop owners tolerated the sale of vegetables and knick-knacks by local farmers and itinerant salesmen.

There was a sports club of modern construction, built outside the village walls for the young people of the village and surrounding countryside, who did a lot of cross-country running, competing with clubs from neighbouring villages, and there were Judo classes that were very popular. Then there was the *Salle des Fêtes*, our community hall, which, like the other recent additions to the village, did nothing to enhance its ancient charms. You had to go round the small back streets or the market square to see real old stone-built village houses, and even there might be shocked to find corrugated iron replacing old tiles, and monstrous picture windows defacing an old façade. The powers that be have now tightened up a lot on what may or may not be done with the façade of an old house, but much damage, I fear, had been done already.

Monsieur Pochon's shop opposite the church was an old house, but masked by large windows and striped roll-away awnings that kept the sun off his fruit and vegetables, which he set out daily on the narrow pavement as the sun rose, and took in as darkness fell, or when he thought it unlikely that any further customers might call.

There was a mangy looking mongrel dog in the shop when I first entered it, a dog with an oversize body precariously balanced on inadequate legs, who suddenly lifted one of them to pee copiously over the pyramid of toilet paper rolls standing in the middle of the shop floor.

Monsieur Pochon, who, like his dog, had short legs, scant hair and peevish eyes, looked over his shoulder towards the door and shouted angrily: '*Sale bête! Vas-t'en, sale bête!*'

He was not, in fact, as I had at first thought, addressing the dog, but a man, who stood in the doorway pulling rude faces at him, and who went off smartly down the road when he saw Monsieur Pochon step down from his hop-up and emerge threateningly from behind the counter.

'At least the dog chose the loo rolls,' I joked, hoping to divert the shopkeeper's attention from the man, clearly no friend of his. 'It could have been over your box of cheese down there,' I added, pointing to the floor near the 'cold' counter, where a box full of ripe Camemberts, already pungent, lay open, waiting to be stacked behind the glass that was supposed to protect the shop's perishables from contamination by over-inquisitive customers.

As a holiday-maker, for some reason I had never in fact bought anything much from Monsieur Pochon, but now I was here for good, I felt that if the choice was reasonable and the prices not too high, then it seemed sensible to patronize the two village shops. Like the post office, the school and the chemist, they kept the village alive. I still had no transport, but was looking for a moped, for it was a long walk to the village.

Monsieur Pochon was clearly not amused by my remark, and asked me in a monotone what it was that I wanted.

'I'm looking for a pot to hang from my pot-hook,' I replied. 'I've only the open fire at the moment, and it's my only way of getting any hot water until I get things organized. I thought you might have a large pot with a handle – preferably black,' I added.

The shop seemed to stretch right down the street. From the main part, which sold cheese and pâté, bread, fruit, ice-creams and fly-swats, dog food, seeds, wine and loo paper, an archway led into a veritable emporium: plastic flowers spilled over sets of saucepans, rolls of chicken wire tangled with kitchen aprons, and doormats vied for floor space with bottles of butane and sacks of fertilizer. It was a wonder that anyone ever managed to extricate what he wanted from this jungle, but somehow Monsieur Pochon wormed his way through it all and, wheezing like an elderly harmonium, pulled out a large pot with a semi-circular handle.

'*Voilà!*' he said triumphantly. 'Was there anything else?'

I hesitated. 'But it's bright orange ... I had hoped for a black one ...'

'My dear lady,' he replied, clearly exasperated that anyone should be so choosy about something so utterly unimportant. 'My dear lady, in next to no time it will be black with soot, so what's the difference? It's the last one, anyway. People don't use them nowadays the way they used to.'

There came a pause.

'Well do you want it or don't you?' he snapped, irritated by my indecision.

Then he tried blandishment: 'I'll tell you what. The normal price is ninety francs. As it's the last, you can have it for only eighty five.'

I had no idea what this sort of pot should cost, but I urgently needed hot water until I could get round to installing something better, so I bought the thing and began to carry it out of the shop.

'So you've bought a house here, have you?' Clearly Monsieur Pochon's curiosity was getting the better of his ill humour. 'Would you be in the village or outside.'

'I'm outside; about a couple of kilometres outside.'

'Now which house would that be, I wonder?' he muttered, almost to himself. 'Pinloup's house, or perhaps the Jeanblanc's old place?'

'It's always referred to as "*La maison Jeanblanc*",' I replied, feeling I must say something. In any case, he would know sooner or later where I lived. It surprised me that he didn't already: surely this village, like all villages, was awash with gossip.

'And do you live there *all alone*?' he asked, looking me up and down over the top of his metal-rimmed half-glasses.

Caution was the order of the day with this busy little man, too curious by half.

'Only on the rare occasions when I don't have friends staying,' I replied, considerably bending the truth, though with little compunction, since he really had no right to question me in this way, and I was under no obligation to tell him my life history.

I found Monsieur Pochon's 'fresh' food counter so uninviting, with its fly-blown glass screen and dubious counter, its slabs of *pâté maison* greying at the edges, and its yogurts whose very pots looked tired, that I have to confess that I did not go there often. He even managed to have 'fresh' bread that seemed to be stale before it reached his shop. So I tended to patronize the other, smaller store, where at least the food was fresher. I did, however, continue to go to Pochon for ironmongery and other hardware, so he did not seem to bear me too great a grudge.

Some very old friends began to come and stay with me for a fortnight or so every year, first with one baby, then with two, and I looked forward to their visits as one of the highlights of my summer. Now, believe it or not, fresh eggs – really fresh eggs – were quite hard to come by. I did not even consider Monsieur Pochon's, knowing what I did of his other comestibles, but the other shop did not seem to do much better. They had trays of variously sized eggs, from which you could take your pick: these had come in fresh that day, they always said, straight from the local farmers. After encountering a number of decidedly old eggs, and even the occasional bad one, I came to the conclusion that free range eggs are a toss-up: the hens lay where they like, when they like, and the farmer may or may not happen on them for days, perhaps weeks. So their freshness cannot be guaranteed unless, of course, you have your own hens in a relatively small run.

I told my friends that I was planning a small hen run, and they immediately said they would like to give me a pair of hens as soon as the run was ready to accommodate them.

So when the following spring came, while the ground was still soft enough after the winter rains, I hammered in some tall wooden fencing posts in a large rectangle round the hen house. This was the back end of a small Citroën van, minus wheels, that the garage man had let me have, into which I had fixed a couple of perches and two nesting boxes just inside the rear doors. All I now needed was chicken wire to stretch from post to post, and I was in business. My friends were coming shortly and we would no doubt be looking for my first lodgers.

So down I went to the village for chicken wire, which Monsieur Pochon managed to disentangle from goodness knows what in the 'Emporium' and brought out, panting but triumphant, onto the pavement along the main road. His wife, her eyes like black saucers, poked her head out of the back room and asked plaintively if he wanted help, but he said he thought his customer was quite able to help unroll the netting for him to measure it. His dark blue overall smelt stale as he stood beside me, and when he took his metal tape from his pocket, I noticed black crescents of grime under his nails and nicotine stains on his fingers.

He laid the roll down on the path and asked me to stand on one end of it to prevent it rolling itself up as he unwound three metres or so. Then, after placing a crate of beer bottles on his end of the netting, he crawled back towards where I stood immobilized on the free end, took a good squint up my skirt and, whistling to himself, began to measure.

At three metres, he made a mark and told me to release the end gently and come and stand at his mark. When I realized that he intended to repeat this procedure as often as he could in order to measure out some thirty metres or so, each time treating himself to a leering squint at my knickers, I rebelled. I stepped briskly off the end of the roll, which sprang into the air and in a flash had done its best to roll itself up again, wrapping itself round his balding head as it did so. He let out a yell, more of protest than of pain, shouting at me to get his head out of the netting and stand on the wire again. Leaving him pinned down as he was, and ignoring his curses, I slowly walked off and fetched a second beer crate with which I eventually managed to immobilize 'my' end of the wire.

'Perhaps it would be easier if your wife were to help you as she suggested, don't you think, Monsieur Pochon? I don't seem to be very good at it.' And, without waiting for his answer, I called Madame Pochon, who came shuffling from her dark back room in her crumpled felt slippers, wiping her hands on her apron and screwing up her eyes as she stepped out into the sunlight.

My friends and I fetched the hens from an old man who lived alone in a large house at the back of beyond. He assured us that they would be good layers and soon adjust to their new surroundings. So quickly did they adjust that, although their legs were tied to prevent them flapping around in fright all over the car, they somehow managed to get from the floor onto the back seat headrests where they perched contentedly as we drove the whole way home, watching, as if to the manner born, as the landscape flew by. By the time they were in the new run and had been introduced to their henhouse, they seemed already to answer to their names: Biddy and Rosie. And from then on they gave me an egg, or even two, every day, and became delightful companions.

But my relations with Monsieur Pochon were not as easy. I often wondered what the scene with the man who pulled faces at him had been about, until I heard the story of the changing room.

The village was divided, so it appeared, into two camps: those who shopped at Pochon's and those who did not. I had noticed that Pochon made much of his easily accessible position, in the very centre of the village, opposite the church, to lure unsuspecting holiday drivers into his shop by advertising cold drinks, *Bordeaux Supérieur*, fresh bread and *'tout pour le camping'* ... His best customers were clearly those who came only once.

When the creation of a by-pass was mooted in the village council, Monsieur Pochon protested loudly that it would ruin his trade. So the by-pass was shelved and through traffic continued to roar round the bend between church and Pochon's, to the consternation of everyone except Pochon. He had fought off disaster once: he would not let a by-pass get the better of him.

That first disaster had been long before my time, in fact so long ago that by no means everyone in the village remembered it. But for those who did, it was still something to be angry about, or something to have a good laugh over, according to one's point of view.

Monsieur Pochon, back in the days when his hair was less mangy-looking, when his overalls smelt fresher, when his daughter was a little girl at school all day and his wife didn't shuffle everywhere in those dreadful slippers of hers, when his shop was new and reasonably clean and there were no supermarkets, and people didn't have cars the way they do now, then, in those balmy days, as well as all the things he sold now, he also sold women's skirts, blouses and dresses.

But you couldn't buy a dress just from the size on the label, could you? And he, who never trusted anybody, was certainly not going to allow his dresses to be taken home to be tried on before they had been paid for. Who knew what they might do with them before they brought them back?

So he arranged a 'trying-on room' upstairs above the shop. For some reason this lone room did not communicate with the rest of the first floor, but was accessible only up a narrow stairway from the back of the 'Emporium'. It would be ideal: they could go quietly up there and try the dresses on, look at themselves in the long mirror he had arranged against one wall, then come down having made a sensible decision, and buy the one they really liked themselves best in.

Only it didn't quite work out like that. Some of the women wanted his opinion, and who was he to refuse such a service? He found himself much in demand: to bring them this or that, to remove something that was not suitable, to do or undo buttons or zip fasteners they could not reach, to examine the hemlines, sometimes even to help them wriggle out of an over-tight dress, which brought his hands into contact with plump, smooth shoulders. He never knew what it would be next, and he lived each day in a frenzy of expectation and excitement at the thought of those half-naked bodies squirming to extricate themselves from a close-fitting dress, of the smell of skin not normally revealed...

Of course there were those who, more brazen than the others, openly offered themselves to him. And who would lose a good client by refusing? Then there were those who needed only very little persuasion. In all, it was a very satisfying time of his life, and profitable too, for he did a lively trade in dresses.

Then one day when he had a woman upstairs trying on a dress, as he was stroking her bare shoulders, he heard people calling for him from the shop downstairs. When he got down, still somewhat flustered, he found himself face to face with a posse of very angry men from the village. Most carried shotguns, one a rifle.

'*Où est ma femme?*' roared the rifleman.

'Your wife?' Pochon replied, 'She's upstairs in the changing room trying on a dress.'

'*Martine!*' the man bellowed, red with rage, '*tu descends immédiatement. Im-mé-di-a-te-ment, je te le dis!*'

Martine did not need to be told twice. She almost lost her footing in her haste to come down the narrow stairs, *immediately*, as her husband had ordered. About her shoulders were draped various garments: an assortment of dresses, blouses and skirts, plus her own dress, which she had snatched up in the hustle and had been unable to get back into in time.

'I've a good mind to shoot you,' said Martine's husband to Monsieur Pochon, whose already sickly face had by now gone a pale shade of green.

Martine screamed: 'He wasn't doing anything! What on earth are you all on about? I was only trying on a dress!'

'I don't care what you were trying on, but you're not trying on anything more – ever – not here, at any rate,' and he led her across the road, past the church and up the long street to their house, just like that, in her petticoat. Some of the old ladies still remember seeing her go by, '*Toute nue,*' they would whisper to one another, cupping their hands round their mouths.

That was the end of the 'trying-on room', and almost the end of Monsieur Pochon's business, since half the village never set foot in his place again, but continued to show what they thought of him by pulling rude faces or singing bawdy songs as they went by on foot, so that the unfortunate man might never forget how much they hated him.

The other half of the village thought it all a huge joke, but of course never referred in any way to what had happened, and continued to buy their hot water bottles and their hair curlers from him.

Monsieur Pochon did not know which group he hated most, the righteous indignant or the hypocrites who laughed behind his back but continued to use his services when they needed them. The only people he could stand were those who stopped on their way to the Pyrenees or to Spain to buy their bread, cheese, ham, wine and fruit for their lunch. He was never called to account for the quality of his food: they simply never passed that way again.

One very hot summer's evening I went down to the store in a pair of Bermuda shorts and a sleeveless T-shirt. It was a mistake, for Monsieur Pochon took it as an invitation to get 'friendly', and, crinkling up his eyes in what he thought looked like a smile, he offered me an ice-cream after I had bought and paid for what I wanted. I thanked him but told him I didn't care for ice-cream, and made off as quickly as my legs would carry me, fearing even to glance over my shoulder in case he was standing, arms akimbo, as he so often did, in the doorway of his shop.

He never forgave me. It was at about that time that he began to vent his spleen on the village by choosing Sunday mornings, when people were attending mass in the church opposite his shop, to roll gas bottles noisily up and down the street, whistling the Marseillaise or singing, in a loud, cacophonous voice, some of Maurice Chevalier's more disreputable songs. Later he resorted to banging two saucepans together, which he said was to call his dog, who chose now to spend his old age at the edge of the square in front of the church, where he no doubt found he got kicked less often.

Walking had become a martyrdom for Madame Pochon, even in her dilapidated carpet-slippers. Her eyes looked as battered as her footgear, and her voice, a plaintive whine at the best of times, was scarcely heard any more at all. Their daughter had brought disgrace on them all, her father said, when she announced that she was pregnant, and he had put a hundred franc note in her pocket and turned her out. He could well have done with her help in the shop now, but was too proud to ask her to come back.

Some weeks after the ice-cream episode I found I needed a few things one Sunday afternoon, when everyone was closed. My friends, on their annual summer visit, drove me into the village and I entered the shop saying '*Bonjour, Monsieur Pochon*'.

But Monsieur Pochon, as usual, was busy on his hop-up, rearranging his shelves, and did not even turn round. So I began assembling what I wanted. When all was collected, and I had the exact money in my hand, I thought the time had come to attract his attention. I coughed. He spoke without turning to face me.

'I'm not sure whether I feel like serving you today.'

'Do as you please. I've collected up everything I wanted. I've added them all up and I don't need any change. I'll just leave the money here on the counter if you like.' And I put the money down and walked out of the shop.

A House Among Vines

Before I could get back into my friends' car, Monsieur Pochon was outside, screaming almost incomprehensibly something about '*les sales Anglais*'. He battered on the driver's door, then, to our even greater alarm, rushed back into the shop and returned brandishing a large green wine-bottle like a club. We did not give him the opportunity to break it on the car, which he certainly would have done had we not by then been able to accelerate out of his reach, leaving him gesticulating wildly with his evil weapon, alone in the middle of the main road, while his mangy dog, used to this kind of scene by now, slumbered on beside the church door.

'Ah, well,' thought Monsieur Pochon, suddenly wondering what on earth he was doing in the middle of a busy road with a bottle in his hand, 'it will soon be the end of July. Just think of all those August holiday-makers going south while the others who've been on holiday this month return northwards! I must prepare some new notices to put along the roadside at the entrance to the village. They're the best customers, they are – here one moment, gone the next! No nonsense with them!' He rubbed his hands together in satisfaction, glanced up at the church clock, and began to carry in the trays of peaches and pears from the kerbside before calling his old dog in and shutting down the shop for the night.

V   Of One Dog and
Three Cherry Trees

Monsieur Pochon's advances were not the only ones I had to
defend myself against, living alone as I did in a house as remote
from others as mine was. I remember once noticing a group of
travelling tree pruners working in a neighbouring orchard and, as
my plum trees had not been touched for some years, I asked them
whether they would be interested in pruning as few as four trees.
They agreed, and we fixed on a price. They would come down to
my place when they had finished where they were, probably
towards the end of the afternoon.

In due course the four men appeared and got to work rapidly,
since the daylight was beginning to fail. The job did not take them
long, for they had a noisy generator from which they ran four pairs
of powered secateurs capable of slicing through branches thicker
than a broom handle.

So as soon as I heard them turn off their generator, I prepared
their money and put it on the kitchen table. It was, however,
always customary to invite people who had worked for you into
the house, maybe to wash their hands at the sink, and usually to
offer them a quick drink of something as you settled up with them.
So, particularly as it was almost dark by then, I asked the four men
in, feeling that at least there was safety in numbers. But instead of
drinking up quickly, they began chatting about this and that:
wasn't it lonely down here? Didn't I get bored sometimes? What
did I do with myself all day? And similar slightly indelicate
questions, which seemed to me to be growing more and more
personal and indeed bordering on the impertinent.

Then they started on about my dog, a gentle black beast who lay
spread-eagled on the matting, her ears twitching at their every

word. She was a *very* large dog, so large that if she tried to walk under the dining table, she would lift it into the air – a most disconcerting performance – but had never hurt a fly, as they say, though I have seen her catch mice as they ran across the kitchen floor, so swiftly could she move when she chose to. Was she dangerous? One of them asked. Did she bite?

At that moment she gave, quite uncharacteristically, a low growl, and I took my cue from her.

'No,' I replied. 'No, she doesn't bite … Not unless I tell her to, of course,' I added after a brief pause. 'I'd only have to say the word, and she'd eat you all alive. She's been trained, you see.'

I had never seen anyone drain a glass as fast as those four men. They were on their feet and out through the door in five seconds flat, while my 'trained' friend gave a short, sharp bark to speed them on their way.

Another small incident occurred when a man I knew only slightly visited me on some business matter – I was doing a little translating to keep body and soul together – and as he was leaving, threw his arms round my shoulders in an attempt to kiss me. Now I was not even on 'social' kissing terms with him, and I certainly did not welcome this advance. But no sooner had I recoiled slightly, as one does, and found myself still in his grip – for he was much taller than me – my dog leapt at him from behind and put her two huge paws firmly on his shoulders.

'I say, get your dog off me!' the man pleaded, cringing in terror, all bravado evaporated, unwilling to move a muscle for fear of further provoking my friend, who continued to lean her considerable weight against his back.

'It's quite simple,' I said. 'You let me go, and she will get down.' So he released me, and the dog jumped down of her own accord. I had never known her protect me like this before, since the occasion had never arisen, but neither had she ever been 'trained', in spite of what I let people think!

A funnier thing happened some time before I had a dog. A neighbour, a peasant farmer I knew only slightly, arrived unheralded at my house one day, just when my magnificent cherry trees were so laden with cherries that I scarcely knew what to do with them all. I had picked all I could reach from ground level, then filled more baskets from my ladder, but there were still thousands of them hanging from branches I simply could not get at, mainly because the centres of the old trees were full of large boughs that prevented me getting the ladder close enough in. And, knowing how brittle the branches had become, I was frightened to climb into the trees themselves in case I had an accident. Had I fallen, with no telephone to crawl to, even assuming I could crawl, I could have found myself in serious trouble. So I took no risks.

The man must have had a sixth sense, or been spying on my activities, for he had come with a large basket, offering to pick my remaining cherries in return for half of what he picked. This is known locally as *faire à moitié*, to 'go halves', the work being paid for with half the crop. Since I realized that the remaining cherries would go to waste otherwise, I accepted his offer gladly.

Now this man was reputed to be *lunatique* – in other words affected by the phases of the moon, and especially disturbed at the full moon. I never quite knew what form his madness, if madness it was, took, but he always struck me as a trifle bizarre, dressed as he usually was in clothes that seemed to have come from another age, almost amounting to fancy dress in our rather unadorned mid-twentieth century. They had in all probability belonged to his great, great grandfather, or even further back, but his wife would tolerate no waste of any kind in their household. If the clothes were there, they were there to be worn, and she was totally uninterested in their style, their suitability or their appearance.

She, for her part, dressed herself, while on the farm, entirely in sacking, and one would glimpse her going about her business wearing skirt, jerkin and a large shawl, all roughly cut from old jute sacks, with strips of jute wrapped round her legs to act as stockings!

She was like the largest of one of those sets of Russian dolls: about the same capacious shape, solidly built, and with high, almost Eastern cheekbones. The skin of her face, naturally quite

dark, always looked as if it had been scrubbed and polished; her
cheeks were round and full like ripe, burnished apples, and she
carried herself as one who had total control over her life and
environment, upright and full of energy. Needless to say, the
family cash went everywhere with her, in a jute bag slung round
her waist, so that she retained the stewardship of every centime
they possessed.

On the rare occasions when she and her husband ventured out
of their domain to visit the post office in the centre of the village,
or for some quite exceptional reason were obliged to go to the
town, some twenty minutes' drive away, she would wear a slightly
faded black full skirt, that reached below her calves; it had three
rows of rick-rack braid round the hem, and reminded me of the
skirts we used to make out of black-out material during the war.
Black boots, a black blouse, a colourful poncho-type woollen wrap
and a wide-brimmed black hat, which she tilted forward because it
would not otherwise fit over her black chignon, conspired together
to make her look like a Mexican Indian. She was indeed a striking
woman.

Her husband, on the other hand, in spite of his outmoded
get-up, was less noticeable. Somewhat timid most of the time,
especially in her presence, he could be affable when he met you, or
pass you by without appearing to have seen you. Perhaps those
were the days when the moon was full.

On that afternoon he was clearly affable, so when he had
climbed each of the three trees, had picked all the remaining
cherries, and we had divided the spoil in two on the kitchen table,
I offered him a drink in the customary manner, and we took our
glasses outside onto the terrace. Then, before he had even touched
his drink, he began to tell me about his wife. How she was a
wonderful woman, managed the place so well, worked so hard,
was stronger than many a man, a paragon, in fact. *But* ... (I had
been waiting for that 'but'!) but, once their daughter had been
born, twenty odd years back, she had consistently refused any
sexual relations with him, until he had eventually given up trying.

'So,' he went on, leaving me no time either to comment or
commiserate, 'So you see I thought that as you too, living alone as
you do, must be starved like me, it would be a good idea if we were
to get together, as it were, when we felt like it, and have a good
time. You see, my wife has told me often enough that I must feel
free to do whatever I like. Unless it costs money, of course,' he

added as if by way of an afterthought. 'That she wouldn't agree to. She's very careful about money, you know. But then you wouldn't want any money, would you? We'd "go halves", like the cherries, wouldn't we?' he concluded, leaning forward with a laugh and giving my knee a resounding slap.

It obviously hadn't even occurred to him that I might not be as keen on his idea as he was, that I might not actually fancy him, or that there might be other good reasons why I might say 'no'. For 'no' it was, but how to say 'no' without humiliating him or hurting his feelings was a real problem. I had managed not to laugh outright at the bit about the money, conjuring up as it had, visions of his wife in her hempen homespun, counting out the francs and the centimes, with such laudable parsimony, from the small jute sack tied permanently round her waist.

I seemed somehow to have managed to convey my refusal without hurting him, or so it appeared. Men are always so vulnerable in such situations, aren't they? Anyway, he finished his drink, collected his share of the cherries from the kitchen with apparent good humour, and told me that if I would care to buy a bottle or two of eau-de-vie that they distilled at home, I could come round one evening with some empty bottles, and he and his wife would fill them for me.

Now distilling is an ancient art, practised in country districts, legally or illegally, from time immemorial. The government naturally sees all alcohol as a source of revenue, and has tried to control home distilleries. For many years registered distillers were allowed to practise their art, and these were able to hand down their 'permit' to their sons. But in more recent times it was decided that home distilling was to die with the demise of the permit holder, and could no longer be transmitted from father to son.

I gave my neighbour the benefit of the doubt concerning the legality of his distillery and paid them a visit one evening as suggested, taking along four clear glass litre wine bottles, as asked, two of which I had filled with tap water and corked firmly. The other two were duly filled with a transparent liquid smelling quite unlike water, and in their turn carefully corked like the others. As I drove off, he said: 'If you meet the gendarmes, tell them that it's Holy Water!' His wife, pocketing my money, gave a sniff of disapproval at his irreverence, and waved me off the premises with an air of relief. He never tried the cherry game again, I am glad to say.

VI   Vines, Plums and Tornadoes

There are a surprising number of English settlers in this south-western corner of France: the Dordogne attracted them (as it did Neanderthal man, for the best of reasons) very many years ago, and now a new generation of them has also 'discovered' the Lot-et-Garonne, the Landes, the two Charentes, and the more rural parts of the Gironde. These *départements*, apart from the Charentes, but including the Dordogne, and the Pyrénées Atlantiques, form the administrative region known as Aquitaine, some of which was called Guyenne before the Revolution (and the name is still used), while another bit, consisting largely of the Dordogne, is still known as the Périgord. Then, of course, there is the term Gascogne, applied rather loosely to the area we think of as South-West France. All of which leads to a certain confusion amongst foreigners. It is a lovely place to live: pretty rather than spectacular, welcoming, especially when the local people find that you can communicate with them, and above all wonderfully uncrowded.

Most of the *agriculteurs* – as they like to be called – in this very rural area are peasant farmers: a few have high quality vineyards, and some of these make quite a good living, especially those entitled to call their wine 'Bordeaux'. It seems anomalous that two vineyards producing the same grapes side by side under identical conditions can be labelled 'Bordeaux' on one side and something far less prestigious on the other, simply because the boundary of the *département* (roughly equivalent to county in England) happens to run between them! The result is that wine growers in the Gironde – the 'Bordeaux' area – are incomparably better off than their neighbours in the adjacent *départements*.

As for the others, who produce a bit of everything (from wheat to rape, maize and tobacco, from apples to kiwi fruit, plums and walnuts, from tomatoes to strawberries, cherries and hazelnuts, and from milk to beef, veal and pork), for them life is both arduous and unpredictable. For not only are they faced with necessary but ill-understood changes to their farming practices, but they have to battle with weather that is perhaps too extreme and capricious for growing lots of the things they in fact attempt to grow.

Of course here the wine-makers suffer too, for while sharp frosts during the winter months are a blessing, as they kill off the various bugs attempting to overwinter among the vines, once the new growth has begun and clusters of leaf buds are beginning to push their way through the reddish-brown winter bark, one hour of severe frost is enough to blacken them, destroying in its wake any chance of a reasonable harvest. The same goes for the acres of plum orchards: a sneak frost in early May when the trees are in blossom will blight that year's plums, ruining any hope of a fat cheque for the prunes they should have become. And of course a single hailstorm during summer will pierce the ripening plums, making it impossible to turn them into those wonderful, soft, sweet *pruneaux* that are one of the specialities of the region.

Then there can be winds. Winds such as one sees but rarely, yet when they come they can lay waste acres of wheat and maize, tear roofs off houses, send huge beams flying several hundred yards, and rip up whole orchards of mature trees.

I experienced wind like that once: a veritable tornado, it came in a black swirling funnel across the countryside, ominous looking. 'Goodness,' I thought, 'It must be absolutely pouring over there!' And in a flash it was on me: the garden table and chairs were flung holus-bolus through the new veranda window, smashing everything in their path. An ear-splitting crash came from the roof above me in the region of the chimney, while the french windows in the room I was in were hurled open, their wooden frame snapped across the top by the sheer force of the wind.

Then for about four minutes the entire countryside flew in at seventy miles an hour and came to rest inside my house. The walls were plastered with slivers of leaves, mashed rose petals and mud. Every picture on the wall opposite the french windows was soaked, each mount revealing brownish stains all around its edges where water had forced itself in behind the glass. I was ankle-deep in it all. The accompanying hail had chopped everything to shreds: huge cuboid blocks of ice that ravaged everything they touched.

Not a single leaf remained on any of my trees, and although it was July, it suddenly looked like mid-winter. The vegetable patch was nothing but a sea of mud, the paint was stripped off the shutters and their wood pitted by the hail. Even my lip was cut, inside and out, by a hailstone that caught me in the open doorway. Thank goodness that it all happened just before eight in the evening, when every self-respecting farmer was inside washing his hands before watching the weather forecast on the eight o'clock news, otherwise, with roof tiles flying in all directions, there could well have been many human casualties to add to the disaster.

It cost over eight thousand pounds to put my major damage right, and I never was so glad to have been properly insured. But the farmers, those who had lost their entire grape or tobacco harvest, whose plums would never make prunes that year, perhaps never again, given the state of their trees, whose handy but dilapidated barns had collapsed, how were they to cope, I wondered? For many of them either could not or would not insure, saying that it cost too much.

There is much real poverty here, while a few live in poverty without good reason. There are still old ladies who, while keeping up appearances when they go out, live in houses where the floors have never been tiled, their scant furniture standing on beaten earth. Only no one ever sees this, until they need an *aide ménagère*, the French equivalent of a home help, and the true level of their poverty becomes known.

It isn't always poverty, though, for one woman I heard of in a nearby village, who actually owned five houses there, was so mean that she refused to let her *aide ménagère* get her one new cup, although all hers were cracked beyond redemption and had become dangerous to use with hot liquid.

And of course I was forgetting one of our village councillors, a farmer, whose 17-year-old son still sleeps in his parents' bedroom (albeit with a curtain round his bed) because they have never got round to doing up a room for him in their excellent loft opposite the bedroom. Neither have they ever done anything about running water, except for a single cold tap over the old traditional stone sink set in the kitchen wall. It is no wonder that their clothes are but rarely washed, when it all has to be done by hand, and all the water they use has no option but to run out through a small pipe in the wall and lie in a most unsavoury muddy pool beside the main door into the house, until it drains into the ground or is dried up by the sun.

Quite soon after I settled in France I got to know my closest neighbours: simple, friendly farmers who lived down the hill from my house. They farmed less than twenty hectares in a fairly basic manner, and, because there were a number of them, and they worked terribly hard, they managed to be pretty self-sufficient. Their vines grew just beyond the end of my garden, and the rest of their land consisted of the hillside between them and me, and surrounded their two houses in the valley below, near one of the roads that runs from the village, and about a kilometre or so from the village itself.

The village of La Motte stands on higher ground, at approximately the same level as my house, but separated from it by another valley. By road it must be at least a couple of kilometres. The quickest access to these neighbours was, in principle, across the fields, but it was not all that easy going, so where possible one would tend to go by road when visiting them. Their name was Boniface: I don't know to this day the Christian names of the grandmother and grandfather, but young Claude Boniface married Thérèse and they had two children, now grown-up, Céline and Charlie. When I first came on the scene Charlie was a toddler. Much has happened since then, and I shall try to recall some of it, for it really does illustrate a way of life that is still to be found down here, a way of life shared by most of the older generation of peasant farmers in this region, regardless of their origins.

VII   Another Way of Life

It had been so hot an afternoon that my daughter, on a visit from England, had joined me with her baby under the huge walnut tree near the corner of the house, and the child was attempting, without much success, to roll off the rug we had laid on the coarse, prickly grass.

There were just the three of us in the house, since at that time – more than twenty years ago now – I lived alone in splendid isolation in this large, solitary house a couple of kilometres from La Motte, surrounded by an acre of land, and was visited from time to time by family and friends.

'Don't you find it lonely?' asked my English friends. 'Aren't you frightened, all alone up here?' my French friends, the females in particular, would inquire, shuddering as they glanced around the big, half-empty rooms and huge, dark barn. My children knew me well enough not to worry about my living alone. And as for the French, I simply told them that the house had its ghosts with whom I lived on excellent terms. They thought me barmy, gave a wry smile and shrugged their shoulders.

Another thing my French neighbours disapproved of strongly was our sitting under the walnut tree. They never, but never would sit under a walnut tree, for fear of I wasn't quite sure what. In the end I came to the conclusion that because the shade from a walnut tree was much denser than any other, one could in fact easily become chilled, unless the air was exceptionally hot. It was true that normally one would not choose the walnut's shade, but there were extremes of temperature that made it the only place to be, unless one remained indoors with the shutters firmly closed.

So we were reading peacefully under the walnut tree, while the baby cooed and babbled and chewed on her plastic ring, occasionally rolling from her back onto her tummy, with a look of intense surprise on discovering this sudden change of view, followed by dismay when she found herself unable to resume her initial, more comfortable, position.

We had been wondering whether the time had not come to think of going in when there was a crackle of dry grass somewhere over near the hazel clump, and suddenly, from behind the fig tree on the far side of the garden, two figures emerged, hot and dishevelled from struggling up the hill with two enormous baskets of vegetables and fruit.

'*On vous apporte quelques fruits*,' the older of the two women shouted across the lawn in a deep, almost masculine voice. Her daughter-in-law merely smiled, and when they reached us, held out a slightly timid hand and said '*Bonjour Madame*,' to me and then '*Bonjour Madame*,' again, to my daughter.

'Aren't you frightened to let the baby lie under the walnut tree? *Elle va attrapper du mal*,' said the older woman, predicting unspecific ailments that followed inevitably upon such a piece of folly.

'We've only been here for a moment,' I replied, slightly bending the truth. 'And in any case, we shall be taking her in shortly.... You haven't brought all this for us, have you?' I inquired somewhat disingenuously, in a rather feeble attempt to change the subject.

'Oh, it's nothing,' replied the younger woman, with a pretty but rather sad, diffident smile. 'Just a few things from the garden – nothing at all.'

We all went into the kitchen, which our visitors clearly preferred to being outside – their lives were spent outside in the fields under a blazing sun, and they found it inconceivable that anyone should choose to prolong the agony – so we sat round the big kitchen table and drank some ice-cold mint syrup, a great favourite with the local ladies on hot days.

I emptied the two baskets onto my smaller working table and was astonished at the rich variety of what they had brought: there were huge white spring onions, green and red peppers, green courgettes and golden *patissons*, some leeks, a few early main-crop onions, a couple of raw beetroot, a cluster of French beans, some fresh haricot beans, two magnificent melons, half a dozen peaches, some nectarines and a few early golden plums.

'Later on,' promised the older woman, 'later, round about the fifteenth of August, there will be the *prune d'ente*, the plums we make prunes from. You must come and see how it is done. You

know, we do our own. They're much nicer when you do them
yourself; better than having them dried at the co-operative, that's
for certain.'

'It's terribly hard work, though,' added her daughter-in-law.
'All that stooping to pick them up from the ground each day. It's
every day for a month. Your back's nearly broken by the end of it.
Some people do it on hands and knees, but the ground is often
rough and you can't move about quickly like that. I don't hold with
it, and anyway, Claude always wants everything done in a hurry,
so he doesn't let us kneel.'

'Quite right, too, he is. There's almost more than we can all do
without anyone slacking,' her mother-in-law retorted with a snort
of disapproval. That her son's wife should have thought fit to
criticize him, however slightly, amounted in her eyes to
lèse-majesté, no less, and could not be tolerated.

Thérèse relapsed into her customary silence, her cheeks
reddened by the older woman's call to order. She was a tall,
handsome woman, not given to expressing her views, since she was
never asked to do so, and she went about her daily round in
silence, often alone, once the children were at school all day, since
her husband worked largely on his own or with his father on the
farm, and took his main meal at noon with his parents, when she
would join them briefly to eat as little as she could get away with
and wash the dishes afterwards.

Claude, her husband, baptized Claudio Bonifaccio, was born in
France – just – to Italian parents who had fled the rise of Fascism
and increasing penury in Northern Italy during the thirties. His
mother had given birth to him, her only son, soon after she, her
husband, their two small daughters, her two sisters, three brothers
and all their families had arrived in South-West France. Her
husband's brother had chosen Chile, where, although penniless
and almost illiterate when he arrived, he had eventually made a
fortune. With the help of their respective wives, the two brothers
continued to write to one another every month for the next fifty
years, although they were never again to meet. The Chilean
brother died in his late seventies, while Monsieur Boniface, as he
was known to the French (who Gallicize every name they can, and
even those they can't), lived on to a very old age indeed,
hard-working as ever to the last.

During the late twenties and early thirties, as I mentioned, the
French government, in despair at the progressive desertion of the

countryside in the South-West of France – a desertion partly caused by the catastrophic losses of able-bodied men during the First World War and partly by the unexplained negative birth-rate among the native Gascon population – offered abandoned farms to families from Brittany and from Northern Italy, on condition that the newcomers farm the land, regardless of their profession or calling before emigration. The result of this policy is still visible, not only in the telephone directories, where Italian names, often only thinly disguised, outnumber French ones in many localities, but in the faces of the immigrants. For Gascons have brown, sometimes almost black eyes, which are rarely lost to the northern Italian or Breton blue, since intermarriage remains the exception rather than the rule.

There is still, I am afraid, an undercurrent of mistrust between the three groups. The Italians, who rank many excellent craftsmen among their large families (six or seven children being still not uncommon), are accused by the Gascons of having 'taken over the country'. The original requirement to farm, and do nothing else, did not prevent a tradesman using his skills on his own farm and handing them on to his sons, who now dominate the building, roofing and woodworking trades, along with those of architects, designers, draughtsmen and painters.

When accused openly by the Gascons of this take-over of 'their' region, the Italians, and indeed the Bretons, who are almost as prolific as the Italians, reply with good humour: 'If the place had been left to you lot, the foxes would have gobbled you all up a long time ago!' After which the Gascons unleash their secret weapon and talk ostentatiously to one another in the market-places in their particular and very localized Gascon dialects, which remain impenetrable to anyone whose ears have not been tuned from an early age to their particular patois.

Claude's mother, *'La Mémé Boniface'* as everyone called her, told me once that Claude did not walk or talk until he was over two, but added proudly: 'It didn't make a scrap of difference, though. He could ride a two-wheeled bicycle by the time he was three, so you see, it means nothing. Absolutely nothing.' As for the talking, it sometimes struck me that he had failed to make such spectacular progress on that front, as his speech consisted, inasmuch as I had ever heard him say anything, almost entirely in monosyllables conveying the most basic instructions to those around him.

Granny Boniface seemed to enjoy talking to me, and especially loved showing me the results of all the work she did: she had two enormous freezers stocked with chickens, ducks, geese, turkeys, partridges, quail and guinea-fowl, all of which she had herself brought up (she always bought day-old chicks in the market and kept them under an infra-red lamp until they were old enough to be introduced to the big outside world of the hen-run). Then, provided the fox was kept out of the run at night, she would in due course cut their throats, pluck them, clean them and preserve them in the appropriate manner.

I was shown her jars of *confit*: lightly roasted chicken, duck, or goose, jointed and then preserved in a large stone jar, a *toupine*, under a deep, enveloping layer of goose fat. When you wanted to serve it, all you had to do was to fork out the joints you wanted and cover the rest over with fat again to keep it air-tight. A few minutes under a hot grill allowed the surplus grease to run off the chosen joints and there they were, delicious and wholesome as if fresh out of the oven.

Then there was shelf upon shelf of bottled fruit and vegetables, including the famous local *cèpes*, golden brown boletus that grow, often to a considerable size, mainly among young oaks after the first autumn rains. Round here people will not even tell their best friends where they had found their *cèpes*, and these fetch exorbitant prices in the markets. I think they are incomparably better eaten fresh, but of course, if you really have too many, you might as well enjoy them in the winter too!

If ever a house made one feel that eating the produce of its kitchen was not only delicious but safe, it was Granny Boniface's house. How she managed to keep it all so clean and sparkling, the floors shining, the table-cloth spotless, the stove looking like new after each meal, I found hard to imagine, for she not only had all her hens and other birds to look after, but had rows of cages full of *Fauves de Bourgogne*, lovely golden rabbits with white underparts, who had to be fed, watered, cleaned out, mated, and protected from the dread myxomatosis as from roving dogs that roamed the countryside in packs during their own mating season, not hesitating to tear open any accessible rabbit-cage and make off with the contents.

Then she had her wonderful vegetable garden from which she fed the entire family all the year round. This was the women's province, like those totally unnecessary folderols women were always on about: their flowers.

'Useless! Waste of time!' Claude would say. 'Valuable land! For nothing!' But his mother would pretend she hadn't heard and went on tending her dahlias, her Arum lilies and her geraniums with the same devotion.

And of course she worked in the fields too, especially at harvest time, struggling with bales of hay or straw as she stacked them high in the upper reaches of the hay barn, ready for when their twelve cows were brought inside for the winter months. They had a few dozen rows of vines, too, from which they made enough wine to see them through the year with a little to sell, on the side, to neighbours and friends. I must confess I did not really care for it much, but they drank it with evident pleasure.

One day Granny Boniface showed me the room that stood across the yard from the house. There, on winter afternoons, they sorted tobacco leaves, rejecting any with holes or other imperfections before they tied them into graded bundles. For, along with their grapes, their wheat, their maize, their sorghum, their sunflowers and their lucerne, they also grew tobacco.

Tobacco was state-controlled, she told me. You had to be licensed and could only grow as much as you were registered to grow. The crop was examined regularly by government inspectors, and insured by the state until 10 October, I think she said, by which time it must all be in to dry. If hail, frost or other natural disaster should damage the leaves before that date, the inspector would order either the stripping off (by hand) of all damaged leaves or, if the damage was too great, the ploughing-in of the entire crop. You were paid the basic contract price, whatever happened – sufficient to cover your expenses – but if the crop was intact and brought in, dried, sorted and duly baled, you earned considerably more, according to the quality of leaf you had produced. I remember one year seeing Thérèse and her two children, Céline and Charlie, struggling on hands and knees along the rows of tobacco, stripping off every leaf, for they had all been damaged by hail, but early enough in the season for more to grow.

When the crop was ripe, it was cut at ground level, stacked by hand on a flat trailer, and brought under cover. Then the elongated heart-shaped tobacco leaves were hung up in bundles along the rafters of the huge brown wooden tobacco barn, with its slatted panels along each wall that tilted as required to allow the air to circulate freely around the bundles.

In the old days, people used to hang tobacco from the rafters in their lofts, but it made their roofs sag, and no one does it any more. The new barns do the job better, and the demand for air-dried tobacco for Gauloise cigarettes continues, apparently, unabated, in spite of ever-increasing price rises decreed by the government, in order, it would appear, to finance the ever-increasing costs of medical treatment for the ever-increasing number of patients suffering from smoking-related diseases.

I was asked to lunch one Sunday, though I could not quite think why. Up to that time I had not been of much help to the Boniface family, and they kept on plying me with fruit and vegetables and other useful items.

Old Grandpa Boniface, *Le Pépé*, grew a couple of rows each year of something that looked like wheat at first, but then branched into a kind of fountain of small stems that spilled out from the tougher main stem, and grew to about fifteen inches long. When these plants were fully ripe, the small seeds were gathered from the ends of the tassel-like top, and the whole thing was cut, upended, dried and bound together, in groups of twenty-five to thirty, with fine wire covered over with split cane, to form a short, round handle beyond which projected the stiff, dry, multiple-headed tops that made an excellent small hand broom. I have yet to find anything better for seeking out dead leaves and dirt from odd corners of terraces and outbuildings.

Pépé hobbled towards me as I entered the yard: he had hurt a leg many years back and had lived with a pronounced limp ever since, though it never seemed to prevent him doing more strenuous work than anyone else in the family until he was well into his eighties. He was as lean as a fencing-post, and held his head on one side to talk to you, which he did volubly, in his Italian dialect from the *Venezia Julia*, which still remained his only language after fifty or more years in France. I understood scarcely a single word of what he said, but we got on like a house on fire.

He waved a handful of his small brooms at me, gesticulating as he spoke, his one good eye leaping around its sunken socket with excitement. I was to take the brooms, I gathered, he had so many … they would keep my house clean … no, he didn't sell them, not to me. And now, *mangiamo* – let us go and eat, I understood, as he pointed a gnarled forefinger towards the back of his throat. I put the brooms into the saddle-bags of my newly acquired but ancient moped and headed for the kitchen where *Mémé* and Thérèse were putting the finishing touches to the lunch.

This involved filling about fifty choux puffs with whipped cream and assembling them into a *Pièce Montée* – a pyramid of profiteroles over which caramel is then poured until it runs like molten lava down the sloping sides. The puffs for this construction had been made by one of Claude's sisters, who, with her husband and three noisy children, was invited like me for Sunday lunch.

Sunday lunch was always a special event, and therefore necessitated a dessert, unlike weekday meals. But this dessert had something even more special about it: three of the profiteroles had been pre-filled by Claude's sister and were reserved for the very top of the pyramid. I guessed they must have some small coin or trinket in them, no doubt for the three youngest children. The three women put the whole thing together, sticking each puff to its neighbour with a tiny blob of caramel, then, with much giggling, poured the rest of the hot caramel over the top and put the creation away in a side room until it was required.

The three men came in from the yard, washed their hands at the sink and sat down without further ado. The five cousins found seats around the huge table, and I was peremptorily ordered – '*Asseyez-vous là!*' – to sit between Claude and his wife. After filling my glass with some unknown apéritif, with the further instruction, '*Buvez!*', Claude filled his own glass and passed the bottle around the table for everyone to do likewise.

I drank a quarter of my glass in one go, but when I put it down on the table again, Claude admonished me: '*Buvez! Buvez!*' And I had to down the rest, like it or not. The soup was served: a thin beef bouillon with carrots and lots of vermicelli, just what my apéritif needed. But when the next course arrived, hard-boiled eggs with mayonnaise, I saw I was not to be let off the hook as easily as that, for Claude had filled my glass – the same glass was used for everything – with wine, his own red, I suspected, and urged me on as before with a loud '*Buvez! Buvez!*'

While the bottle was being passed round, Claude got up from the table and crossed the room to a point beside the fireplace where an enormous ham hung, closely wrapped in a white linen bag, from one of the larger beams. Ceremoniously, he untied the drawstring at the bottom of the bag, pushed it upwards out of his way, took out his folding pocket-knife, and began to cut long, thin slices off the ham, which he handed down to his mother as she stood beside him holding a large dish to receive our next course. This homely version of Parma ham was served with bread, radishes and butter and was quite delicious.

Then we ate sliced, cold beef with carrots and gherkins; probably the beef that had made the excellent bouillon. And more wine, glass after glass, accompanied by shouts of '*Buvez! Mangez! Mais buvez donc!*'

Ordinary conversation appeared impossible, since Claude seemed only concerned with whether I was eating and drinking enough, while Thérèse was visibly overwhelmed by it all, and hung her head in silence over her plate, taking as little food as possible, although I noticed that she filled her glass regularly. Granny Boniface seemed to be the only person I could have made real contact with, but she was too far away and too busy serving her meal to be of any help, so I resigned myself to just eating, drinking as little as possible, and smiling at anyone who seemed likely to smile back.

Next came the main course, or so I thought: a kind of ragout, or stew, known locally as '*La Sauce*'. It was guinea-fowl – *pintade* – usually a trifle dry when merely roasted, but quite delicious served in this manner, the thick sauce bringing out the full, slightly gamey savour of the bird. The wine continued to flow, and I had to admit that it made an excellent accompaniment to this course. Following everyone else's example, I too accepted a second helping of guinea-fowl, without needing any encouragement to 'eat up!' from Claude, although he seemed to be programmed to repeat his litany at set intervals, regardless of whether I was eating, drinking or slacking on the job.

Then, to my horror, Granny Boniface opened her oven door and brought out the most succulent leg of lamb I think I have ever seen. Crisp-skinned on the outside, and very slightly pink inside, its sweet juices ran into the dish as she cut slice upon slice until the whole joint lay in pink and redolent layers, waiting for our appetites to revive. I cannot claim to have been hungry still, but the flavour of that lamb remains with me to this day, married as it was with a huge bowl of fresh green beans, lightly cooked and tossed in butter before being sprinkled with the merest soupçon of garlic and most of the juices from the lamb. Once again I was obliged to empty my glass, since the principal meat dish is always served with a bottle or two of '*Vin Vieux*', good quality labelled wine of respectable age and origin.

Things became noisier after this, as Claude required the television news to be switched on, and the children, who by now were beginning to race round the table between courses, skilfully dodging their various parents' ill-aimed slaps as they careered past the points of greatest danger, added their shouts to Claude's sporadic cries of '*Buvez! Buvez!*', and the news at full volume topped it all as the roar of Sunday football crowds and the horror of multiple motorway pile-ups enlivened the general festivities.

Cheese was served, home-made, taken fresh from the small plank that ran between two beams high up, close to the kitchen ceiling. It did not have the flavour of the full, rich French cheeses, but was 'interesting', I think one says. Perhaps more reminiscent of Edam, that pale cousin of the Dutch Gouda.

And then ... and then ... the *Pièce Montée* was borne in, all a-crackle with caramel and oozing with cream. The children were suddenly glued to their chairs again, watching like so many hungry puppies as the pyramid was ceremonially taken apart. Because Claude was the most important person present, or so his mother thought, he was given the top three puffs and the rest were swiftly shared out until we were all poised to take our first bite.

I noticed that Thérèse looked across at her husband for the first time since the beginning of the meal, and that Claude's sister was watching him slyly, trying hard to keep a straight face. His mother's expression was bland, revealing nothing, but she was looking at him, nevertheless, as he picked up his first cream puff and bit generously into it.

There was a pause, and the picture of Winnie-the-Pooh's friend Eeyore biting on a thistle suddenly filled my mind's eyes, as I saw Claude spit out the remains of his first mouthful in horror. He reached across in front of me, and deposited the uneaten half on his wife's plate, with a roar that drowned even the din from the television.

'*Mange! Mange!*' he bellowed, and I saw Thérèse collapse with mirth and cover her face with her hands, while everyone else screamed and roared their amusement till the tears ran down their faces. A furtive glance at the 'cream' puff told me it had been filled with mustard.

After all that wine, laughing like this just about finished me off, and I had to ask Thérèse where one went to *faire pipi*.

Now an elderly English lady of my acquaintance once told me that she would rather burst than ask a French hostess if she could use the loo. Thérèse gave me a slightly odd smile, blushed – but then she often did – and pointed to the door with the latch at the back of the kitchen.

I had been shown the three other rooms that led off the kitchen, but never been through this particular door. Naturally enough, I thought: one does not usually include the loo when showing visitors one's house.

Making my way across the room as inconspicuously as possible, or so I hoped, I lifted the latch and found myself face to face with twelve huge *Blondes d'Aquitaine* and their four calves, who greeted the appearance of a total stranger with loud mooing and stomping of hoofs.

They were, fortunately, tethered, the calves in the darkest corners of the barn, the cows each to her own stall, with her name written on a card pinned to the oak above her head, along with the date of her being taken to the bull.

The space between the back of each cow and the wall was just about wide enough for me to feel safe from a well-aimed rear hoof as I crouched in the straw to spend a penny, before making my return to the relative civilization of the gentle plop-plop of an electric coffee-maker and the blare of the television set, still hopefully competing in the corner of the room.

It was five o'clock and time for me to make my way home, wondering how I could possibly repay the warm and unusual hospitality I had just received.

VIII Hay, Prunes and a New-born Calf

I did not have to wait long, for during the following week the *Mémé* Boniface asked me whether I could drive a tractor. I had to admit I never had but was ready to have a go if it would help.

Charlie drives the tractor now, for better or for worse, but in those days he was too young – his legs did not reach the pedals – so I did my best with the decrepit old faded red Massey Ferguson. I cannot help thinking with some nostalgia of those far-off days when Charlie was still a little boy and I would spend long afternoons with them all under a blazing July sun, slowly coaxing the temperamental old tractor along while the women and children gradually gathered the whiskery green bales of hay into a semblance of a straight line, and the men hoisted them one by one on the end of very long pitchforks to the top of the ever-growing pile on the trailer behind my back. There the indefatigable *Mémé* stacked them higher and ever higher, until she herself was finally marooned one and a half storeys up, and had to remain precariously perched where she was, as our procession swayed its gingerly way back to the barn, to begin unloading into the cool darkness of the hay-loft.

I would help with the off-loading too, and that was not only back-breaking work but left you covered in scratches that would itch all night long and for days afterwards. These were worse when we had to handle straw, and I soon realized why the older local women, who always dressed in skirts and never in trousers, would nevertheless don an old pair of their husbands' cast-offs under their skirts when it came to dealing with hay or straw!

They co-opted me to plant tomatoes and potatoes, to gather up plums for prune-making, to pick strawberries and the tomatoes I had helped to plant. I have done many a *vendange* with them, whether in the rain or the blazing sun, and partaken of the generous meal that is always served on such occasions, to spur on the workforce to greater efforts until sundown brought us in, exhausted but happy.

It was from the Boniface family, the old *Mémé* in particular, that I learned much about how to grow my own vegetables, to keep hens, bantams and ducks, and to breed rabbits. They welcomed the plums from my few trees and dried them for me in their old round brick oven with its cast-iron doors. But first I had to arrange them on the slatted wooden *claies*, shaped like elongated pears, or, as some have suggested, like snow-shoes, which were then fitted like the petals of a flower on the circular shelves of the iron trolley, before it was wheeled along its rails into the oven. The fire had to blaze for a couple of hours until only red embers were left: it was then that you put the plums in, and they remained there until the following morning, when the whole procedure was repeated again and yet again for a third time. On the final morning I was told to come down with my prune jars (huge glass preserving jars with screw-top lids), eighteen lumps of sugar for each jar, and whatever alcohol I wished to preserve my prunes in. The prunes came hot, and still slightly soft, out of the oven and went straight into the jars with their sugar and alcohol. The lids were screwed on firmly and a solemn injunction given not to touch them for at least two years. I still have a few that must be at least fifteen years old and they are marvellous!

Visitors from Britain often ask me what alcohol I used to preserve the prunes, since they almost always assume it is done in very expensive Armagnac. Of course you can buy prunes in Armagnac, and indeed do them yourself like that, but if you are prepared to wait sufficiently long before broaching your home-bottled prunes, ordinary *Alcool pour Fruits* is all that is needed, and that can be found on the shelves of any supermarket around prune-bottling time, and costs infinitely less than Armagnac!

I wish all my memories of the Boniface family were as happy as these, but, alas, I was to be the sad spectator, over the years, of the kind of family dramas that seem to occur all too frequently, and about which I, as a stranger, could do nothing.

IX Thérèse

Thérèse, Claude's wife, was a strong, handsome, big-boned woman, the sort of woman who stood out among the small, round-shouldered, dumpy Italian women who seemed to take over the market square on Fridays, our local market day. Madame Boniface, her energetic mother-in-law, thought her sullen. She would stand there, she said, and stare at you, with those high red cheekbones of hers and a ghost of a smile on her lips, until someone addressed her in French, then she would smile more broadly, but rarely answer. Of course you couldn't expect a girl from the Poitou to be able to speak the same language as everybody else, that is, everybody they knew.

She had always been against her son marrying someone who wasn't Italian, but you know, he'd always had a will of his own, that son of hers, and Thérèse it had to be. So that was that. Of course, at first she couldn't understand a word of what they were all saying, so Claude did his best to translate for her from the *Venezia Julia* dialect they spoke together at home.

One of her married daughters had teased Claude at lunch one Sunday. Asked him how the two of them managed to talk to one another in bed. Her brother was furious. Scarlet, he went. She thought he was going to burst, and his speech became even more incoherent than usual.

'*Parler! Parler! Pas b'soin d'parler!*' he roared. Whenever he shouted, which was often, it was always in French. '*Le taureau, pardi, i'parle pas, lui!*'

Once he had managed to get the words out, Claude sat back in his chair and beamed proudly at the assembled company, delighted at his own fluency. Then he bellowed with laughter at his own wit and thumped the table with pride, making plates and glasses rattle.

Madame Boniface *Mère*, though decency forbad her to laugh at jokes about bulls not needing to talk when mating, thought that her son's clever reply was just what his sister needed to put her in her place. Thérèse, she noticed, was looking down at her plate, her eyes lowered, her cheekbones on fire. She never did join in when they were all together, like on Sundays. Did the dishes after the meal without a word. Just that enigmatic half-smile, as if she couldn't ever wipe it off her face.

When the young couple's first child was born there were great celebrations, although Granny Boniface made it clear to Thérèse that she would have done better to have produced a son and heir for her son Claude. But the little girl would no doubt be given a brother one day. They had plenty of time.

It was six years before Charlie arrived to keep his sister Céline company. Granny Boniface was in raptures over the little man who would carry the Boniface name into the twenty-first century. The fact that he was slower than Céline had been was of no concern to her, although she noticed that Thérèse looked at him quizzically when he failed to respond to her mothering as Céline had always done.

'My son never walked till he was over two,' she told Thérèse for the umpteenth time, when Charlie still lay burbling in his cot while other children of his age seemed to be already running around and talking. 'But you see, there's nothing wrong with him now, is there?' she went on, flashing a quick glance at her daughter-in-law, whose half-smile never wavered.

Charlie learned to walk before he was two and a half and simultaneously to thump other children in a blind rage when they did anything to displease him, or indeed, when they didn't. His aunts refused to bring his cousins to the house any more, but his grandmother considered that the cousins were, more often than not, to blame, and that her son's son was acting as any normal man would when provoked. Meanwhile Céline kept out of his way as best she could, and was thankful that in their shared bedroom Charlie still slept in a high-sided cot.

The little boy was sent to the local nursery school at the age of three, like all the other children in the area, but it was not a great success. During his second term, his teacher called on Thérèse, and told her that all was not well.

'You see, Madame Boniface, I'm frightened for the others. He is so violent – perhaps a trifle less so this term – but much rougher than he should be. And he doesn't seem to want to join in anything, like when we all sing together. And when we do painting, he just rushes around and wrecks what the others are trying to do.'

Thérèse's smile had paled; her strong hands were clenched so tight that the knuckles stood out like bare bones.

'I'm ever so sorry to have to tell you this: I know what a shock it is for a mother, but I do think he should be seen by the school doctor with a view to finding a special school for him. Somewhere where he can be allowed to progress at his own pace. I sincerely think it would be better for him, you know. Talk it over with your husband, won't you? I know he's a busy man at this time of the year, but I'm sure he will be able to help you to understand that what we advise will be in Charlie's best interests.'

Thérèse's worse fears were being confirmed. And yet neither Claude nor her mother-in-law seemed to have, or want to have, the slightest inkling that there was anything wrong. How could she tell them what the woman from the school had just said to her? How could she ever get them to listen? They never spoke to her. They never asked her anything about anything. She was just there, that was about all. She wished the teacher had spoken to them herself; she could not imagine how she was going to tell them.

'I had a visit the other day,' she began haltingly, about a week later, emboldened by a small swig of Cognac from the bottle in the sideboard before joining the others at her mother-in-law's house for their daily lunch. Charlie, of course, like Céline, had his midday meal in the school canteen. It would be easier to talk about him when he wasn't there.

'Oh yes?' sniggered her husband, eyeing her quizzically. 'Fernando, I guess,' he went on. 'And what did he want, I wonder, when my back was turned? You never told me, did you?'

'No, it wasn't Fernando,' Thérèse replied almost inaudibly, her cheeks scarlet. Why did he have to insinuate such things? Everyone knew Fernando had at some time or other had it off with almost every woman in the village. How difficult it was to speak to him about anything, and her mother-in-law didn't help, just staring at her with those eyes of hers like twin black snails.

'It was the teacher from the nursery school. Charlie has to go to another school.' Her voice dropped to a whisper. 'Where he'll fit in better.'

'She said that! And you let her! Charlie not fit in? I'll knock her head off when I see her. Should have called me. I'd have fixed her!'

Claude's face was purple with fury. Then his mother added: 'He's right. There's nothing wrong with the boy. Nothing. Just you wait and see. It's the school that gets him worked up. He's perfectly all right when he's here on his own. We understand one another, Charlie and I do. Not like some people who are always looking for trouble with him.'

And that was that as far as Granny Boniface was concerned.

But the school wrote to the parents: a formal letter that Céline had to read to them, as Claude was not much of a reader and would not trust Thérèse to do so.

After the customary preliminaries the letter told them that the school doctor would be visiting the school on Friday 4 March and would like to examine their son, Charlie. It was important, it said, that they should be present on this occasion.

'You can go,' said Claude to his wife, 'I'm not. Too busy. It's all nonsense. And don't you let them touch him. He's all right. He's my boy. He's all right.'

The doctor had a child psychiatrist with him, and together they considered the reports on the boy, then tested him with some coloured rods, some pictures and some toys. They got him to draw and tried to talk to him, but he either could not or would not speak, and started thumping the little table and kicking the doctor's legs.

In the end they explained to Thérèse that he would be much happier in a school where he was under less strain. That there was no way that he could keep up with the other children of his age without constant frustration, and that this was causing the outbursts of violence from which he suffered. That he would be much better in a special school for slow developers, which he would be able to attend as soon as he was four. Meanwhile it was considered advisable for him not to continue at the ordinary nursery school.

So Charlie stayed at home for the rest of that school year, then went to the special school, taking the school bus that passed the end of their road at seven thirty and getting back between five and six in the evening. It was a long day, and he never seemed to be learning anything, but he was calmer at home and his cousins began to come again to visit without too many upsets.

Neither Claude nor his mother ever again referred to the

nursery-school fiasco, but went on firmly believing, or at least managing to convince themselves, that all was well.

When Charlie was seven, his grandmother thought he should make his First Communion, as was customary in the Italian villages she and her family had come from. Our local priest thought it very young, the usual age in France being nine or ten, after a minimum of two years' catechism. But when he saw Charlie and realized that he would find it impossible to cope with the sort of preparation the other children received, he thought it would be best to treat him as a special case and allow him, for better or for worse, to join the older children who were to receive the Eucharist for the first time in June.

Father Julio came to see Charlie most Saturday afternoons that spring, in the hope that something he told the lad might get through. He talked mainly about how much God loved him, and how he should love God and everyone he knew. He talked to him about the baby Jesus who had been born a long time ago, and who had been sent by God to save us all, though here he wondered what this concept could possibly mean to young Charlie, who, more often than not, seemed to latch onto a single word, and repeat it like a rune as he ran in tight circles around the small patch of tired grass beside the kitchen door, kicking up the pebbles he had just scattered over it.

'*Bébé, bébé, bébé, bébé, bébé, bébé* ...,' he chanted, while Father Julio sat silent on the small bench beside the door. God would, he felt sure, listen to this child, even if his prayers were unorthodox, to say the least. The Almighty had a special place in his heaven for the simple-minded.

One morning as I was feeding the hens, Thérèse appeared through the hazel clump at the back of the hen-run. She had never been to my house without her mother-in-law in all the years I had known her, and indeed, since Granny Boniface did all the talking when they came together, I could scarcely say I knew Thérèse at all, except from what I had observed.

Her habitual shyness seemed to have evaporated.

'*Charlie va faire sa Première Communion le 8 juin. Vous étiez au courant?*' she blurted out, her face ruddier than I remembered seeing it for some time.

Yes, I had heard he was to make his First Communion, but had not known the date.

'Are you going to have a party afterwards?' I asked, knowing that baptisms and first communions were always an excuse for a great family get-together, not always in keeping with the preceding religious ceremony.

'Yes, indeed. You see,' she went on, 'I want to have the lunch at our house, not at Claude's mother's. Not that she doesn't do things well – she's far better than me at these things – but I'd like to feel it was my family party, not hers. Do you understand what I mean? You don't think it's silly of me, do you?'

'But of course not. Will some of your family be able to come?'

'Yes, I hope so,' she replied. 'My brother and his wife and boy – he's about the same age as Charlie – and maybe my mother, though she suffers from depression a lot and I'm not sure whether she'll manage it.'

'Oh, I'm sorry to hear that; let's hope she will feel well enough. It would be nice for you to see some of your own people, wouldn't it? They're from further north, aren't they?'

'Yes. From Angoulême. Not all that far, but it seems another world.' Thérèse replied, and went on with a rueful grin. '*Angoulème, c'est pas l'Aquitaine.*'

It was true that her French was much closer to the French I had been taught to speak. She was no Gascon. It must have been a nightmare for her to come to live in a part of France where she was not herself understood and could not understand others properly. And to add to that, to find herself surrounded in her new home by Italian dialect speakers who made no concessions to her and consequently treated her more or less as an idiot. No wonder she never opened her mouth. And yet I could see a quick intelligence there, a charm and gentleness that seemed absent from her rough-hewn husband and sharp-tongued mother-in-law. Only the old *Pépé*, Grandpa Boniface, with his gammy leg and his funny eye that obliged him to hold his head on one side when he spoke to you, he alone seemed to radiate good will to everyone he encountered. He would have taken up the cudgels on behalf of Thérèse, had he been capable of speaking French. But he had never really needed to make the necessary effort, since his energetic wife had always been the one to make contact with the world outside their farm, and at home they continued to speak to one another as they had always done.

I sensed Thérèse had come for more than a chat, and volunteered: 'You know, if there is anything I could do to help, do please say, won't you?'

She blushed to the very roots of her pretty auburn hair. 'Well, yes. That's what I came to ask. Would you be free on the day to give me a hand with the meal, especially with preparing the room? You know, our house only has the three rooms: the kitchen, which isn't really big enough, and the two bedrooms. If we put all the furniture from our bedroom through into the children's room, we could set up a long table on trestles diagonally across our room, and I think we could manage like that. What do you think?'

It was amazing how she had everything worked out, almost to the last detail, and of course I said I would do whatever was needed. It was clearly a matter of great pride to her that the day should go well. When she kissed me good-bye before setting off down the hill, the heady tang of her breath made me realize that she must have been at the wine in the *chai* to fortify herself before clambering up through the fields to ask for my help.

The eighth of June dawned bright and sunny and I hastened down to Thérèse's as soon as I could, after feeding my hens and rabbits and locking up the house. Charlie was over at his grandmother's with Céline, the children's two aunts, his uncles and their offspring, preparing to make their way along to the village church, as soon as the bell began to ring. Even Claude, who normally considered he had more urgent things to do than go to church, was dressed in his best clothes and seemed to be going along too, proud as a fighting cock of his young son in his hooded white surplice and plain wooden cross.

Thérèse's mother had not been able to come; she was going through a bad patch, Thérèse said, but did not elaborate. Her brother and his family were expected at any minute, though he had made it quite clear that no one was going to lure *him* into a church, she told me with a grimace. She had forgotten about his strongly-held Republican views that allowed no truck with priests and their ilk. But he *was* coming to the party.

There was no way Thérèse and I could join the others, for there was an enormous amount to do before they all arrived back. Thérèse had prepared as much food as possible in advance, but there was the room to get ready, the table to erect and lay, seating for everyone to be found, the salad to prepare, the avocados to halve, stone and fill, the wine to put out.

Together we heaved the mattress from the big bed into the

children's room and leaned it against the wall, then dismantled the bed into its many parts and took those through as well. We decided the wardrobe would have to stay, but we managed to inch it into a corner where it would not be too much in the way. Then the table was erected, board upon board on trestles, covered with four large tablecloths, and a bench from the *chai* put along one side. The garden bench had to be brought in too, and as many chairs and stools as we could lay our hands on. If we had counted right, there were to be eleven adults and seven children. So we had just enough seats for everyone. I was to help Thérèse with the serving, so she and I planned to sit on stools as near the kitchen door as possible.

There appeared to be food cooking, to judge by the appetizing smells that came from the oven, and I let Thérèse get on with that side of things, confining my help to what she specifically asked me to do. She seemed to have to rush around a lot, disappearing to the *chai* for this and that, for it was a large building on the end of the house and, in addition to the wine-making equipment and storage vats, it seemed to serve as a depot for everything that had no obvious place elsewhere. It was only after her fifth or sixth visit to the *chai* that I felt I should offer to go and fetch whatever it was she required, so that she could attend more easily to the cooking. She thanked me with her usual smile and said it was all right, she was managing, but I caught a glimpse of her embarrassment before she went out yet again, and wished I had never spoken.

Thérèse's brother drove up to the house on the stroke of twelve. His wife, forty-ish and rather colourless, clearly did not think much of the farmyard, rough with pebbles and dusty as it was, and teetered cautiously across to the kitchen door, examining her stiletto heels for damage when she reached the safety of the tiled floor. Their son, Rodolphe, a fidgety, hyperactive child, took off at a run, arms flailing, on a tour of inspection of house and garden, to return to his parents, scarcely inside the door out of the blazing sun, where he announced that there were no *cabinets* and where was he supposed to *faire pipi*? Thérèse waved vaguely in the direction of the nearest row of vines at the back of the house, and Rodolphe went off with a palpable air of disgust.

At about 12.30 the others began to arrive back from the church, and when all the greetings were over and everyone was seated, the aperitif was poured. Rodolphe insisted that at eight he was perfectly old enough to have an *apèro* like the adults, so his parents poured him half a glass. Of course, Charlie, whose party it was supposed to be, jumped up and down to indicate that he wanted one too, and his other cousins, seeing which way the wind was blowing, chimed in: 'We-ee wa-ant an *a-pé-ro*; Wee-ee wa-ant an *a-pé-ro*', until their parents thought it wasn't worth trying to say no.

Thérèse asked her guests if they were hungry, as she began to serve the soup. Charlie shouted *'Oui, oui, oui,'* louder than anyone else. His Angoulême uncle began to tease him, saying he couldn't be hungry: *'Tu n'as pas faim. Tu viens de manger le Bon Dieu.'* Charlie looked at him wide-eyed and repeated *'manger Bon Dieu'* and his uncle, unable to resist letting everyone know where he stood as far as religion was concerned, went on: 'So now you've eaten God, we shan't be troubled with him any more, shall we? And a better world it will be for all of us, don't you all think?'

Rodolphe thought his father very funny, shouted *'Oui! Oui!'* and laughed for a good three minutes, while the others sniggered politely, and swilled down the last of their aperitifs. Bottles of wine were set along the table and everyone's glasses filled while Thérèse and I brought on the avocados.

When Thérèse served the *Coquilles Saint Jacques* I noticed her mother-in-law give a sniff of disapproval, no doubt at the idea that any part of the meal had been bought, rather than prepared at home, for she knew Thérèse could never have prepared these delicate scallops in their shells without her knowing about it. But Thérèse was past caring to-day what her mother-in-law thought, and smiled on regardless as the party grew more noisy and boisterous with every bottle of wine they downed. The roast veal, their own produce, was done to a turn, and the peas, freshly picked from the garden and cooked with baby onions, were given top marks by everyone. There was a good selection of cheeses to please all tastes, some soft, some blue, and some hard, and most people took some of each.

Then, before the champagne and the traditional *Pièce Montée*, ordered from the local *pâtissier*, everyone gave Charlie his First Communion presents. Suddenly the table seemed to explode with parcels small and large, prettily wrapped and be-ribboned, and Charlie, understanding nothing of what it was all about, began to tear at the paper wrappings until they were shredded fine over all the table and the contents exposed to his bemused gaze.

One of his father's sisters gave him some rosary beads, which he donned as if they were a necklace; the other, a pen and pencil set in a leather case. His grandparents offered him a missal; his parents gave him his first watch, while Céline had wrapped up a large red ball, thinking that this might divert his attention from kicking the gravel.

Then Rodolphe, prompted by his father, produced their offering, a record of the latest hits, in a sleeve picturing Brigitte Bardot in her prime walking naked along a beach. Charlie's father grabbed it and, staring goggle-eyed at the ravishing intruder, shouted above the general hubbub that she was 'starkers'.

'*A poil*! *Elle est à poil*!' and everyone screamed with delight.

Then, as the champagne corks were drawn and the cream puffs of the *Pièce Montée* distributed, the men, with much laughter and many a jibe, passed the record round to one another for closer scrutiny while Charlie intoned his latest litany: '*A-à-poil, à-à-poil, à-à-poil,*' and his sister and their five cousins joined him in a rousing, tipsy chorus.

'Do you think they enjoyed themselves?' Thérèse asked as we began to clear away the mess. 'Did they have enough to eat and drink?'

'Oh, surely,' I replied. It was six o'clock and everyone had gone over to Granny Boniface's house, mostly on foot, although Rodolphe's mother insisted on being taken by car down the one drive and up the other, for fear of damaging her shoes. We who lived in the heart of the country knew better than to wear shoes like that.

We did the dishes and put the bedroom to rights in a couple of hours. Then Thérèse picked up the record. 'You know, I nearly invited Father Julio. I wonder what he would have thought of my brother,' she added with a giggle. 'And I wonder what poor little Charlie made of it all,' she went on, and as the giggle turned suddenly to a sob she hid her face in her hands and broke into a fit of uncontrollable weeping.

I had never seen Thérèse weep before, and was never to see her do so again. Somehow she must have deadened her craving for understanding and affection by regular doses of alcohol, mainly in the form of the wine they produced so liberally themselves and that was so easily available all the year round, on tap as it was in the *chai*. No one missed the odd litre when they were drawing it daily anyway and had three cylindrical storage tanks, that almost reached the roof timbers, full of the stuff.

Her husband was, in spite of his mother's adulation, less intelligent than she was. He was not a bad or unkind man, at least he did not set out to be unkind, but his rough, homespun nature could never marry properly with his wife's finesse and perspicacity. And since in their world, the man was always right, Thérèse found herself caught in a trap from which there was no possible escape. Except alcohol, which did something to deaden the pain.

Of course, her mother-in-law's beady eyes had soon seen what was happening. She was not a bad women either, and a great deal more intelligent than her adored son. But she had warned him about marrying outside their own circle and had been right. Thérèse was a foreigner, poor stock, she now considered, to judge by her blasphemous brother and her mad mother.

'This so-called depression that Thérèse's mother appears to suffer from is just plain madness, you know,' Granny Boniface told Claude one evening when Thérèse had gone to bed with a headache and he had gone across to sit with his mother while she shelled peas for bottling. 'She has to be locked up from time to time, I gather. You want to watch it with Thérèse, my boy. Keep her on the straight and narrow path, that's my advice to you.'

One day when Céline had reached the age of sixteen and had finished at the agricultural school where she had been a weekly boarder since the age of thirteen, she told her mother that she no longer wanted to have Charlie in her room.

'But Céline, where else can he sleep? We only have the two bedrooms. What do you expect me to do?' asked her mother.

'I don't care what you do, but I won't have him in with me. He's too big. He messes me about when he thinks I'm asleep, he does, and says horrid things.'

'But Céline, he's only ten! I'll talk to him and tell him to leave you alone.'

Thérèse was embarrassed at the turn of the conversation, and knew there was no point in trying to talk to Claude about it. So she chose a moment when she and Charlie were alone and told him his sister did not like the way he was behaving towards her. He seemed not to understand her, though a stubborn little glint appeared in his eyes, replacing the usual non-reactive, apathetic look she had grown so used to.

When Céline complained again, his mother decided she had

better put Charlie in a small bed at the foot of theirs where they could keep an eye on him. She did not even try to tell her husband why, knowing full well that he would simply refuse to believe anything she said, so she merely announced that as Céline was a young woman now, she should have a room of her own, and he accepted the new arrangements with a few grunts as his only protest.

Another problem arose in the form of Fernando, their neighbour from the farm further up the road, who for some reason seemed to be haunting the place. She had quite a soft spot for Fernando, because he knew how to talk to women. His mixture of charm, good manners and the most boldly outrageous propositions seemed to be what they liked, for they succumbed with enthusiasm to his advances.

Here he was again now, appearing as if out of nowhere and when you least expected it – come to borrow this tool or that piece of equipment, to bring a bunch of early carrots, or the latest piece of gossip. He had a gift for moving unseen through the vines, sheltering still as a statue behind a tree, easing his way along a hedge so that he was upon you before you had even detected a rustle on the hillside behind the house. How persuasive he could be, how evocative of the two or three occasions he had encountered her, as if by accident, up in the vines, and, knowing full well that Claude had driven his mother into town that morning, had turned his most potent techniques of seduction onto a sun and wine-drenched Thérèse, to their mutual considerable satisfaction, as he never ceased to remind her.

All that had been some time ago, and she had done her best not to lay herself open to these assaults, knowing how hard she would find it to refuse him when he always made it out to be the most natural thing in the world – her life was difficult enough without wantonly risking further disasters.

So she wondered for a while why he was hanging around the place again, and really wished he would keep away and leave her alone. She would have to make sure that she always had one of the children with her, and not send Céline off to work on her own, leaving herself unguarded to face Fernando's blandishments. Then the truth dawned.

'Oh, no! He wouldn't! Not that!' she suddenly blurted out. The sheet she was folding, fresh from the line, fell to the ground.

'Oh, but wouldn't he?' she breathed, and her heart gave a

sickening lurch.

What was it that Gaston had said about Fernando? 'Anything from nine to ninety.' She used to think that Gaston was just being funny. That he was probably jealous. Now she suddenly saw things in another light.

She stumbled over her half-filled basket, scattering its sun-bleached contents across the yard in her haste to clamber up the hill to where her daughter was summer-pruning the vines to allow the sun better access to the ripening grapes. Claude had gone off to get some part or other for the tractor. Charlie was with his grandmother. In any case, no one could see their vines, the ones at the top of the slope, unless they were up there. And even then ... *she* knew all about *that*.

Céline was cutting away at the dense fronds when her mother reached her. Thérèse was panting and her heart was thumping so hard she could hardly speak.

'*Mais, qu'est-ce-que tu as, Maman*?' her daughter asked, resting for a moment from her work to eye her mother's disarray.

What, indeed? Well might she ask what was wrong!

'Oh, nothing much,' she replied, her eyes scanning the rows of vines for the slightest tremor. 'I just found the hill more tiring than usual, I suppose. I thought perhaps as it was so hot, you'd like to call it a day and come down and have a cool drink. Come on, you've done enough for this afternoon. You're not used to working outside for long hours yet.'

'What do you think we did at school then? Stay all day in our classrooms? We were there to learn how to be farmers, not pen-pushers!' she rejoined with a laugh.

In fact Céline had learnt not only to prune vines, drive and repair tractors, plough a straight furrow, and keep livestock; she could also write a good business letter, fill in tax and VAT forms, and keep accounts. Her father was going to do anything to keep her at home doing all the things he was unable to do. And she, her mother, was going to have to never let her out of her sight again, unless of course some furious husband took a pot shot at Fernando. Otherwise she would have to marry her daughter off as soon as possible.

September came, and with it the promise of a good *vendange*. The thermometer went down a few degrees and everyone breathed more easily. School began again for Charlie, though it seemed more a way of killing time, since he never seemed to learn anything, his mother thought. He was beginning to grow tall and strong, too strong, she sometimes felt, when he grabbed her by the wrist or butted her with his head.

One Sunday afternoon, after lunch was over at Granny Boniface's and the dishes done, Thérèse had gone back to her house and was sitting for a moment on the bench beside the kitchen door, when up their drive walked Monsieur Dupont, their dapper little neighbour from the small villa opposite the end of their drive. As he expressed a wish to speak to them both, Thérèse ran across to her mother-in-law's to fetch Claude, who followed her back reluctantly, none too pleased at being torn from the television.

Monsieur Dupont clearly considered his mission important, since he had dressed in his best suit, a spotless white shirt, a tie, and even wore a waistcoat, in spite of the weather.

Claude and Thérèse could scarcely say that they knew him, for although he had lived opposite them for a number of years, and was always perfectly friendly, he kept himself to himself. He did not appear to work, at least nothing that Claude would have called work, but seemed a bit too young to be retired yet. So when he began to tell them all about himself, they wondered what had prompted this sudden intimacy.

'You see, I have a good, regular income, I own my little house, which is very comfortable, and, well, to tell the truth, I would like to marry ...'

Thérèse held her breath. Surely he had not come to ask for Céline's hand in marriage? The idea was utterly preposterous, yet she could see no other reason for his being here like this, in his Sunday best, too. Poor old chap, he must be out of his mind. Whatever would Céline think of this proposal, a man older than her own parents? However much she wanted to see Céline marry, this was not what she had had in mind. The poor old thing. How could they manage not to hurt his feelings? It would be awful to offend him, to hurt his pride, to make him a laughing-stock. They must be very, very careful how they replied.

'... So I wondered whether you would consider allowing me to propose marriage to your daughter Céline?'

So there it was. She saw Claude start, then draw himself up to his full height. He had not seen it coming and had been caught unprepared. She put out a restraining hand, hoping against hope that he would do his best to be nice, or at least polite, to the old chap. Her husband pushed her hand away brusquely, mistaking it, no doubt, for hesitation on her part, and exploded, spluttering in fury, outraged at the sheer presumption of anyone, let alone this dandified pimp, of anyone wanting to take his daughter away from her parents. He needed her at home.

'*Foutez-moi le camp*! Get the hell out of here!' he said, raising a threatening fist. 'And don't you ever come near this house again! The very idea! Céline marry *you*! You must be mad! In any case, Céline isn't marrying *anyone*, not if *I* have any say in the matter. She's staying here. At home. We need her.'

So from then on, whenever any of them crossed Monsieur Dupont's path, he would look neither to right nor left, but pass on his way as if they did not exist. Thérèse's heart bled for him. He had made himself so vulnerable. But Claude had no inkling of how other people could be hurt, had he?

Céline remained at home, helping her parents, and Thérèse saw to it that she was never alone among the vines. Charlie by then was bigger than his sister, who was small and wiry, while he grew tall and broad-shouldered like his father and seemed to have the strength of a bull. When she was seventeen he crept up one day behind her in the hayloft, where she was throwing down bales for the cows below, and tossed her onto her back in the hay, pinning her under him until she screamed. She said nothing about this episode – what was the point? But it was then she made up her mind that enough was enough. She would start to look for a husband, whatever her father thought, and leave home as soon as possible.

She was lucky. She ran into Pascal, who had been at school with her, though she had not known him well, since he was a year older. But she knew him to be a nice, friendly chap with a slightly deformed foot that he made light of. Furthermore, he was clever and would make a good farmer. He had just obtained his driving licence, and suggested they might go together to one of the local *bals*. Indeed, he said he would fetch her that very Saturday evening, though not before nine, as he had work to do, as always, on the farm. Céline regarded this as quite normal: after all, she too had work to do most evenings until about nine.

It was a streamlined romance, for Céline knew her mind. She must get away from her home, from her poor brother's importunate harassment, from her wine-bibbing mother's growing depression, and, most difficult of all, from her father's increasing tendency to get her to do everything, since, as he said, that was what he had had her educated for. Furthermore, he wanted to hear nothing of Pascal, and all talk of marriage was cut short by a sharp call to order.

'You're too young to marry, and in any case, I need you here!'

So she and Pascal, who was as much in love with her as she was with him, decided on their strategy and set about with much enthusiasm to put it into action.

They did not have to wait long before their plan was seen to be working, and together they went to see Father Julio to ask him to bless their betrothal. This was not something he had ever before been asked to do, but it seemed a reasonable request, so, with a firm injunction to remain chaste until they were married, he gave them his blessing.

Did they reckon to be marrying soon? He asked. And what did their parents have to say about it? Surely, Céline was under age and would need her father's consent. Céline replied that under the circumstances she did not envisage much of a problem. And Pascal's parents were delighted at the idea of such a suitable and charming daughter-in-law, even if she did come from an Italian family.

When the two young people told Claude and Thérèse that Céline was four months pregnant and that their engagement had been formally blessed by Father Julio, Claude was left speechless. As for Thérèse, her relief was obvious, although she felt overwhelmed with unhappiness at the thought of life at home without Céline's cheerful companionship.

'And where the hell are you going to live?' Claude roared, when finally he regained the use of his voice.

'That's all organized,' Céline replied firmly. 'You needn't give it another thought, *Papa*. Pascal's parents are busy converting the end of their house into a self-contained unit for the three of us. We'll come and see you, you know. We shan't be that far away.'

There was nothing for it but to accept things as they were and to plan the wedding, which took place with great pomp and ceremony a couple of months later. I still have the printed menu for the superb meal that was served at a local restaurant, where we all danced till the small hours. I thought Thérèse might have shed a tear, but she didn't, when the young couple slipped away, as is the custom here, to the supposedly secret hide-out where the first night is to be spent. (Never a well-enough kept secret, however, to stop the revellers descending on the newly-weds, a couple of hours later, bearing a soup tureen full of *tourin*, the traditional garlic broth said to induce fertility ...) No, she just sat there with her fixed half-smile, looking somehow diminished, as if shrunken, dried up.

Life went on, however, much the same as before, though Céline's help was sorely missed. Granny Boniface continued to get through more work in a day than almost all the other members of the family together. Charlie learned to drive the tractor, though after he once drove it at his mother, who only just managed to jump clear, she avoided working too close to him. Claude, who had seen what had happened, assured Thérèse that it had been an accident, that the boy's foot had slipped, or something. But she had seen that glint come into her son's eyes. It had been no accident, and she felt increasingly ill at ease with this huge, graceless young man who now towered over her like a misbegotten giant.

At the appointed time, Céline gave birth to twins, a boy and a girl, who had gone to full term undiagnosed and surprised them all. Then a year later, she had another little girl, followed by a boy two years after that. At each baptism there was a big family party organized by her parents-in-law, to which her own parents, brother and grandparents were naturally invited. Thérèse was pleased to see what a good mother her daughter seemed to be making, and especially to see her so happy. Pascal adored his children as much as his wife and seemed to Thérèse to personify the perfect husband.

Back at home, her life seemed to be all work, and her almost total lack of communication with her husband or his parents began to make her wonder what she was doing there. Her son caused her increasing anxiety. Her mother, whom she never saw, eventually died, under circumstances she was never fully able to elucidate. Depression, they said. Madness, said her husband, though she didn't ask him how he was supposed to know, when no one would tell even her what had really happened.

'And if you're not careful, that's how you'll end up, too! Just like your mother!' Claude said to her, one day when she tried to tell him of her anxiety about Charlie.

'I just don't understand you,' he went on. 'Charlie helps me a lot now he's fully grown. We get on well. There's nothing wrong with him, you know. It's all in your mind. When I'm gone he'll be able to manage the farm quite well if he gets himself a good wife. You just invent worries. It'd be a damn sight better if you drank less,' he added over his shoulder as he strode out across the yard towards his mother's, refusing to listen to another word.

He had never before referred to her drinking, and she had thought that he simply hadn't noticed, the way he seemed not to notice Charlie's odd behaviour and strange appearance. Now it seemed that he was blind only to what he didn't want to see. Just as his mother's son would always be perfect in her eyes, so would Charlie be in his. She knew that every attempt to convince the two of them that there was anything wrong would inevitably be met with a wall of total incomprehension. She was alone in a desert. There was no point in calling for help, since there was no one to hear.

When her son went for her in the hayloft one terrible afternoon, she was unable to defend herself, such was his brute strength and sheer weight. Then when he grinned at her, like the child he had once been, she ran off in terror and shame and locked herself in the *chai*.

Claude and Charlie found her there later that evening, after they had eventually managed to force the lock. She was hanging from a low beam, her feet twelve inches off the ground, a double twist of black binder-twine round her neck. The bench that lived in the *chai* lay on its side beneath her feet.

'*Pauv'Maman, Pauv'Maman, Pauv'Maman, Pauv'Maman*,' intoned Charlie, as he ran round and round the *chai*, kicking at the earth floor with his shoes.

'Yes, poor Mummy,' replied Claude. 'Mad, just like her own mother. Must have been in the family. Poor Mummy.'

There was a terrible inevitability about Thérèse's death, and an utter feeling of helplessness on my part. I had seen so much of what was wrong, yet could do nothing, any more than anyone else could have done, to prevent this tragedy.

X Bianca Castafiore, or how to be taken for a ride

At first after my arrival I had found my house warm and welcoming. The summer was beginning and I had much to do to make the place more comfortable for my first winter there. I planned a simple bathroom in a small corner of the barn that seemed to have been made for the job, and after purchasing a white bath, basin and bidet, found a very young man who, while still serving his apprenticeship in plumbing, said he was capable of installing them, and willing to do so for an extremely moderate sum, provided I did not mind his working at night!

I accepted this arrangement on condition that he did not expect me to stay up too, so for four or five nights he would arrive at about nine in the evening and work through till I knew not when, for at ten I would go to bed while he worked away until he had finished what he wanted to achieve that night, then would slip away into the darkness. His plumbing was irreproachable: a beautiful job very well done, that never gave me the slightest trouble. Then all I had to do was to tile the floor over the pipework and in due course tile and decorate the walls. It was luxury indeed to have a proper bathroom!

During those few nights I found it quite comforting to know that any noises I heard in the house most probably came from my young plumber, and I realized that I had been slightly on edge when the time came to go to bed: I would often read late into the night, thus postponing the moment when I finally gave in to sleep. An old house creaks and groans as its timbers move with changes in humidity or temperature, and, of course, the barn and the loft were great places for mice or even larger creatures, I sometimes suspected. There was a huge barn owl that visited my open barn, and screech owls sometimes sat on the beams in the loft above my bedroom and squawked like a lot of giggling girls.

So when my old neighbours up the road, Fernando's in-laws, offered me a couple of black and white kittens, I took them in gladly, knowing that hitherto all untoward noises from the barn or loft could be comfortably laid at their door. Zig and Puce soon became indomitable climbers and I slept a lot better from then on.

But the house definitely had a presence in it: not in any way a threatening presence, but a presence of which I was often aware. Not anything I ever saw, either; just the feeling that I was not always alone. I had not at that time heard the Jeanblanc boys' story about their younger brother who had killed his young wife and himself at the house, and was by no means a believer in ghosts of the classic ghost story variety. But the presence continued to accompany me, unobtrusive but there, for several months after I came to settle in the house. It was as if generations of former occupants wanted to make themselves known to me, before fully accepting me as one of them.

Then one day I suddenly felt an overwhelming and totally un-characteristic urge to write about the house and the people who had lived there before me. I shall never know why, but it had to be a poem, and it had to be in French. Quite a tall order, unac-customed as I was to doing either, since I had written no poetry since my teens, and never in French, where the rules of prosody are confusingly different. But I struggled on for days, it seemed, until I had something I liked, something that really represented for me, at any rate, my deep feelings about the house and its former inhabitants. It had been terribly hard work, but I felt reasonably satisfied with the result. And strangest of all, from that very day, the presence I had felt in the house seemed to have gone. I was never to sense it again.

It was about then that Gaston suggested that I should get a sheep to keep the grass short and avoid the constant mowing that was becoming the bane of my life. People who are only familiar with well-tended suburban gardens do not realize how vital it is, in the deep country, to keep nature at bay, and to surround a house with at least a small rectangle of short grass or well-kept flowers, even beyond any terrace or paved area there might be. A house can be overrun with weeds and invaded by tendrils in next to no time, so one has to do constant battle to prevent such a misadventure.

So he and Eliane put me in touch with a family that had a young ewe for sale, and I bought her, paying for her, as the custom was, by the kilo. She was very white and rather pretty, as sheep go, and made very loud bleating sounds when, as I thought, she was not happy, which seemed to be all too frequently. I called her Bianca Castafiore, after the headstrong, strident opera singer in one of the *Tintin* books.

Now the people from whom I bought her told me that sheep should not be allowed to get really wet, and that when there was heavy rain, and indeed at night, I should tether her under cover in the barn. I must admit that I knew little about sheep, but had always thought that they lived permanently out of doors, on Welsh mountain sides and the like, without coming to any harm. But apparently French sheep were different. So I bought her a red leather collar and a long chain with a screwed spike on the end to fix firmly in the ground, so that she had a large circle of grass to crop before I was obliged to move the spike.

Now Bianca Castafiore soon learned that by running in circles round my legs as soon as I began to approach her, she could effectively shackle me with her chain, sometimes even throwing me to the ground, and she seemed to derive a smug satisfaction from so doing. But I *had* to approach her whenever it rained, to bring her in under cover. To make matters worse, she rapidly grew far too big and strong for me to be able to lead her by her collar. She could pull me over and drag me across the garden if she felt like it, which she did more than once with evident delight. So I had to work out some other way of getting her from garden to barn and back again when the rain stopped.

I found that if I straddled her and gripped her flanks between my knees while holding on to her collar, I could gradually shuffle her towards the barn. It was a bit like riding a diminutive pony, but with my weight still firmly on my feet. I then found that the insides of my knees, or of my jeans, if that was what I was wearing, were thick with lanolin from her fleece by the time I had got her indoors, and that this was very hard to get off. So I was obliged to keep a special pair of trousers for moving Bianca, and change into them every time I had to do it! Life began to centre round her and the weather, so that I hesitated to go out if I thought it might begin to rain. It was all completely ridiculous.

Then to add to the farce, I found that sheep never eat long grass when there is any possibility of reaching a short-cropped lawn, so all my hopes of getting Bianca to keep the orchard tidy evaporated, and I had to mow first before she would deign to look at her new pasture! Then one day when I was out, she got loose on my shrubs and bulbs, ending up with a massacre of all my geraniums.

I finally decided to find a buyer who would undertake to breed from her, rather than slaughter her, and this made our parting easier. But when she was weighed, this time in my presence, although she had doubled in size since I acquired her, her weight was apparently the same as when I had bought her. I don't know how much Gaston knew about the people who had sold her to me, but clearly they had seen me coming, as they say. I learned a useful lesson, anyway.

After Bianca had gone to her new home, I decided that rabbits were what I needed, since with one breeding pair it was possible to fill a dozen cages in a few months: the whole thing then takes off in an exponential curve if you are not careful. Living alone as I did, I reckoned that one rabbit would keep me in protein for a week. And my garden was full of carrots and onions and tomatoes, so I could eat braised rabbit with its vegetables as often as I liked. For rabbits, fed on selected grasses and given some herbs before they are killed, make wonderful eating, quite unlike anything I had ever had before. So it seemed a good idea.

My first male was a huge New Zealand White called Kiwi – what else? And his mate, a *Fauve de Bourgogne*, golden with white underparts, I named Alice. Sixty seconds or less in Kiwi's company, and Alice, thirty days later, would produce a litter of eight or more, who themselves were ready for mating in three months!

But the trouble was that I became enchanted with the delightful ways of my pretty rabbits, and in particular with their family life: the mother cares for her babies with intelligence and total dedication, which could not fail to endear her to me, and of course the first litter, from which the females were to become breeders, were all given names to match their already quite marked personalities, as soon as they left the nest their mother had built, and started to run around the cage. Not a good idea when you want to eat some of them.

All this, of course, added up to the fact that I could not bring myself to kill my rabbits. I had steeled myself to do it, and had acquired a gadget that promised to stun the rabbit so that it felt no pain when you slit its throat. But the wretched device, a kind of captive bolt, was almost worse than useless, and I could have spared myself the expense.

In the end, out of sheer cowardice, I offered a supply of rabbits on a regular basis to the local charcutier, who would come and fetch them every other week. And whenever I saw him selling rabbit pâté in the market, I moved quickly on to the next stall. A bit of extra money was welcome, but I was happier after I finally gave them up.

There was worse to come, though, when I thought I would buy half a 'home-bred' pig. What I did not know before agreeing to buy was that the buyer *must* attend the killing, so that there can be no doubt that the pig, or part thereof, that you contracted for is in fact the one that you take home.

So there I was on a frosty February morning, warming my hands at an alfresco fire in a small back yard of a house in the village, where I had been told to come for the ceremony. The pig, all unawares, was grunting softly in his 'home', a stone structure built onto the back of the house, just big enough for his now huge girth, where he had spent his entire life in the process of getting fat. As he was led out by his owner, a rope tied round one of his back legs, he blinked at the early morning sun and yawned, stretching out his hind legs as he did so.

The *tueur* (killer/butcher) had arrived and was sharpening his knives. The *maie*, looking like a long wooden coffin with slightly sloping sides, stood in a corner with two chains lying across it, while a large pot hung over the fire, boiling up the water we were going to need to get the bristles off the animal.

The pig's owner tied the rope round the second hind leg. The pig began to squeal, finding himself shackled in this undignified way. Then the owner, after throwing the rope's end over a large pulley high up on the wall, began, without further ado, to hoist the now shrieking animal up by his hind legs until he was clear of the ground. I would have given anything not to have been there. But I had to go through with it now.

It must be said that they wasted no time at this stage, but every second was a second too long in my book. The *tueur* plunged his long knife into the pig's neck at the level of the carotid artery and slit his throat. The pig stopped shrieking, squealed pathetically once or twice, gave a deep gurgle, twitching convulsively, then fell silent. A large bucket was produced to collect the blood, which then had to be kept stirred more or less continuously until we were ready to start making the *boudin*, a form of black pudding greatly prized in these parts.

Once the blood had all drained, they brought the pig down and laid him in the *maie* over the long chains. Very hot water was poured in around the body and we had to take turns at pulling the chains backwards and forwards to scrape off the bristles. This is quite an arduous task, and in spite of there being six of us – four strong men and two women – it took over an hour to get the bulk of the bristles off.

By now the poor creature looked a bit more like what you see in the butcher's window, and was hoisted once more up against the wall. A piece of wood about four feet long, notched at intervals and slightly bowed, was stretched between the back feet to hold the legs apart while the butcher began to eviscerate then cut up the animal.

By lunch-time the carcass was divided, the gut washed out to make a skin for the *boudin* and any sausages we might want to make, the liver and other offal divided between the two buyers, and we were ready to go home to begin the real work – preparing this huge pile of meat for the freezer, and making all the bits and pieces into pâté. Nothing is wasted from a pig, they always say, and since it can be fed, for its entire life, on scraps, it is really one of the most economical ways of feeding a family. So it is not surprising that almost every rural French family still keeps a pig, or even two: one for themselves and one to sell. And, unlike cows, calves or sheep, the pig may still be slaughtered at home as their peasant ancestors have done since the birth of history.

The pork turned out to be excellent, of course. But I had to switch off any connection my mind attempted to make with that gruesome February morning. And as I grow older, I find that meat figures less and less on my menus, to the undoubted benefit of both my body and my mind.

XI Monsieur Pierre

Up in the village the 'Café de la Place' stood on one side of the *Halle*, or covered market square, and was run by a charming old tippler and his pretty wife Henriette. There they served coffee and the usual drinks a bar can provide. But if you wanted somewhere that provided meals as well, you could go to 'Chez Fanny' in one of the back streets. It was cheap and good, and as I was living on my own, I used occasionally to treat myself to a meal there, with or without friends, partly for a change of scene but also because one kept abreast with what was going on in the area.

For after a period in which, although profoundly happy, I scarcely met a soul, in which I came to terms with my situation and communed, as it were, with my house, meeting only those who came to see me, and venturing out as little as possible, I had become more and more captivated by the rich mosaic of characters that surrounded me and found I wanted to know more about them.

So, as my fascination with my new environment grew, I began to go out more, and where better to go than to 'Chez Fanny'.

It was a warm, friendly place in those days, and it was there that I encountered Monsieur Pierre.

He was always called 'Monsieur Pierre'.

I never did find out what his surname was, nor for that matter, whether Pierre really was his first name; it was simply a question one would never have asked under the circumstances, even though I came to know him quite well as the years went by.

He was the sort of man who made you feel, however briefly, that you and above all, your ideas, were of genuine interest to him. He would face you squarely, look you straight in the eyes, while his sparkled with joyous amusement, a look of connivance that made speaking your thoughts easy in the knowledge that they were perfectly in tune with his.

Handsome, soberly elegant without a trace of affectation, his hair grey at the temples, he must have been in his early fifties when I first became aware of him. He always wore a well-cut suit and a tie, which in any case would have singled him out from the usual crowd at Fanny's, with their open-necked shirts, their jeans, jumpers and trainers.

After all, 'Chez Fanny' was just the village café-restaurant, the only one remaining for several miles around, and therefore much appreciated for all it had to offer. Apart from serving coffee, croissants and drinks of all kinds, Fanny ran a *Dépôt de pain*, replenished every morning by an itinerant baker from the nearest small town. She kept a stove burning in the bar during the winter, and while her more rustic customers warmed their feet on its enamelled top, she would listen to everyone's problems, and learn all the gossip of the surrounding countryside. She also cooked meals so copious and succulent that people working in the area would flock there for lunch. 'Look at the cars,' Fanny would say. 'That's the way to tell where you get good food!'

Not that it was a conventional restaurant; most people in the back room ate at a great long table, with enough of Marcel's wine in pitchers down the middle to be accessible to everyone. The food was borne in through the narrow doorway from the kitchen by Fanny herself, a steaming dish held aloft in each hand, her face red from the heat of her stoves, wisps of fine, coppery hair escaping from beneath the white cotton cap she always wore when she cooked, her dimpled arms freckled and bare to the shoulders, revealing neat, reddish tufts in the armpits as she carried her creation in triumph to the table.

The men at the long table would always be seated and ready as twelve struck. I never understood how they managed it, since warming the clock is not generally a French habit, but there they were at twelve sharp, and Fanny always had the food ready. She would hover over them as they tucked into her *civet de lièvre* or her *veau à la crème*, refilling the pitchers as necessary, bringing on mounds of sweet-smelling bread, sometimes a drop of cognac 'on the house' to help the coffee down on some special occasions. Then they would suddenly notice the time, rise almost as one man and, with much handshaking, stream out joking and laughing through the bar into the sunshine of the village street.

There were a few small tables in the back room too, but their occupants often arrived later than the workmen and were given a choice of dishes. The room would suddenly appear hushed after the men at the long table had left, and odd scraps of conversation, some in French, some in English, became sporadically audible.

'I'm sure I've seen them somewhere around here before.... Surely, that must be old Jack.... No, don't look now, but Mrs You-know-who is with someone I've never set eyes on before....' It was, of course, largely the English who said this sort of thing, the French being much more interested in talking about the quality of the food and making sure their children were 'eating up' properly.

As I ate there myself from time to time I came to know most of the 'regulars', by sight at least, and of course came to hear, or overhear, much of the local gossip. But there was one couple who remained a mystery to us all. They only seemed to come to Fanny's every other Saturday for lunch, or so I thought at first. And although they smiled and greeted everyone with quiet courtesy, wishing us all '*Bon appétit*', he, with his thoroughbred suit and air of distinction and she, with her smiling, sunny eyes and vivacious manner, remained an enigma. Where were they from? And why come here, to the very depths of the country for lunch on Saturday? All Marcel appeared to know about them was that he was called Pierre and that he called her Sylvie.

At Fanny's they always sat at the same small table, very slightly apart from the rest of the guests, as if encapsulated, living in their own hermetic world, absorbed with one another. They appeared to talk a great deal, but so quietly that no one could ever catch even a single word of what they said. They seemed to know one another very well, as they always appeared perfectly at ease together. Their eyes met often and lovingly, but their hands behaved with the utmost propriety and never, but never strayed from their alloted half of the table.

I was invited by an old acquaintance, Jack, about whom you will hear more, to a meal at Fanny's one Saturday night and to my surprise found Monsieur Pierre and Sylvie at their usual table. Perhaps they came for the week-end, but in that case, where did they stay? Fanny's was not a hotel.

Fanny herself eventually revealed that she had 'done up' a spare room specially for them, that they came every other Saturday before lunch and stayed until late on Sunday afternoon before heading off in the general direction of Bordeaux. More than that

she did not know. But she liked them both very much and their
visits were the highlights of her life.

'Such a change!' she said. 'Such a change from the usual
rough-and-tumble and country bumpkins! Now he's a man with
style, he is, and she is ever so nice. Not quite in the same class as
he is, but ever so nice, she is, really. Of course, she's so much
younger. It's hard to get her to talk, though, except to him during
meals, and doesn't he half lap it all up? You can see that he adores
her, can't you? You know, no one else ever uses that room; it was
done up for them and theirs it's going to remain. I couldn't let
anyone else use it, could I, when it means so much to them. No,
that's their room for as long as they want it.'

I had not often heard Fanny so loquacious, except when she was
scolding Marcel, though even then she would more often than not
sulk at him if she had cause to feel cross. She had reached an age
when she seemed to need to be constantly reassured of his
affection for her, and showed signs of jealousy when he joked and
laughed with women customers. A blind would be pulled down
over her usually cheerful face and she would go about her work
tight-lipped and uncompromising. It cast rather a gloom on a visit
there if you happened to catch her on one of those days.

An English neighbour of mine, looking for a house on behalf
of someone else, heard from Marcel that there was one for sale
nearby, which he volunteered to show her, an offer she saw no
reason to refuse. They visited the house one summer evening,
after which Marcel called in at a cousin's who insisted, with typical
local hospitality, that they both join the family round the kitchen
table for a chat and '*un petit blanc*' – some of his excellent white
wine from grapes grown on the hillside behind the house.

The evening stretched on. Darkness fell. When eventually
Helen was returned to her own car outside Fanny's, the shutters
were closed over the café door and a general air of gloom hung
about the place. She assures me that Fanny was never quite the
same towards her since that innocent but unfortunate evening.

The years went by and Sylvie, who must have been scarcely out of
her teens when she and Monsieur Pierre first started coming to
Fanny's, began to take on the mature confidence of the early
thirties, increasingly radiant and self-possessed. As for her
companion, he never seemed to change – a wisp or two more of
greying hair, perhaps, but what matter? Still the same attentive,

loving solicitude for his adored Sylvie. Always the perfect gentleman, considerate, polite and totally discreet, yet with that relaxed charm and warmth characteristic of the well-educated upper echelons of French society.

Some English friends, more frequent visitors to Fanny's than I, planned a party for one Saturday night, and asked Fanny whether she thought Monsieur Pierre and Sylvie would care to join them. It was then that Fanny told them in a burst of confidence what little she had managed to find out about the couple.

'Monsieur Pierre is the head of a big family business in Bordeaux, I gather. You know, lots of money but not much time to enjoy it. And Sylvie came to work for the firm, oh, straight out of school, I should imagine. He fell in love with her; "*le coup de foudre*" it must have been', she explained, pointing heavenwards as if to reinforce her belief that thunderbolts could, and did, fall even from the most limpid summer sky and make two people, whom man would not have thought of joining, fall helplessly and irrevocably in love.

Sylvie had continued to occupy the same humble niche in the firm and not a soul had ever suspected her relationship with Monsieur Pierre, so discreet was their public behaviour. His wife, of course, must have known, or at any rate guessed, that his disappearance from home every other weekend indicated some regular assignation, but since it evidently made him happy and easy to get on with, and was above all clearly being conducted with the greatest possible discretion, and he continued to treat her with the utmost courtesy and affection, it had never seemed right to her to want to probe any further.

Although my small corner of France is well under two hours from Bordeaux by car, for anyone living in that busy city it must seem as remote as the Garden of Eden, with its gentle hills and valleys, its quiet rivers and myriad streams, its dense woods of oak, acacia and hornbeam dotted with pine and spruce, and its vineyards trimmed like neat hedges on every sun-baked slope.

Outside the small villages, large square farmhouses – one third living accommodation, two thirds barn – their shuttered windows facing east and south, their westerly aspect well battened down against the autumn gales, stand half a mile or more from one another in the midst of their vineyards. Some are long, low buildings, accommodation for humans at one end and barns for cattle, hay and wine at the other. Occasionally the *chai* – in which wine is made and stored – has been built apart from the house and, from a once simple, homely, rather grubby, dark area with a beaten earth floor and huge rectangular concrete vats for storing the wine until it is bottled, it has gradually been modernized: stainless steel cylindrical vats and impeccable tiled floors become a necessity once your neighbour has them, and there is now never so much as a cobweb in sight.

Living conditions have also changed dramatically in the area, and the local people sing the praises of the British, who have brought their love of home comforts to the region and 'taught' (their word) the French to restore their old houses gracefully. Whereas twenty years ago the farmers were abandoning their old farmhouses in favour of poorly built, mean bungalows, once they began to sell the old buildings to the British and discovered what it was possible to do with them, those who still lived in their old houses set about transforming them with considerable success. Bathrooms were put in, so that great-granny no longer had to lift her skirts over the straw of the cow-barn, or crouch, come rain, hail or snow, among the vines. Kitchens were modernized, floors tiled and polished, insulation was installed under the roof so that rooms could be added upstairs, where once the onions used to dry. Tobacco is no longer hung from the roof trusses but occupies its own ventilated barn, and home-made cheeses no longer dry on planks suspended from the kitchen ceiling beams. A loss, perhaps, but what an immense gain in comfort it has all been for those who endured the earlier primitive conditions.

Yet in spite of the changes, it is still a place where people have time to stop and talk, where indeed it would be unthinkable not to do so; a place where Bordeaux is a foreign land to be visited only *in extremis*. For apart from its excellent hospitals Bordeaux has nothing to recommend it to the local village people. So what could have been a better choice for Monsieur Pierre and Sylvie than 'Chez Fanny', not even advertised as a restaurant, let alone as a hotel? Where almost all who ate and drank there were regulars and could therefore be counted on not to have any potentially compromising connections with Bordeaux. Monsieur Pierre and Sylvie themselves became 'regulars'; their relationship was never questioned, and no one showed the slightest interest in what they did for the other five and a half days of each week. Their secret life was safe here.

They accepted the invitation to the party. Sylvie looked lovely. Once her initial timidity was overcome, her increased self-assurance enabled her to enjoy talking to other guests, most of whom spoke only rather halting French anyway. Monsieur Pierre was delightful: a highly sophisticated and intelligent man, he had a wide range of interests and spoke most entertainingly about them. We discovered a common knowledge of Spain and similar tastes in music, but after a while I became aware that our fairly animated conversation was being met with anxious glances from Sylvie across the room, and Monsieur Pierre, forever the gentleman, went over to keep her company for a bit. The evening went well on the whole, and everyone seemed at ease. I noticed how adroitly both he and Sylvie would steer the conversation gently away from any inadvertently indiscreet question; not that the other guests would have deliberately embarrassed them, since they had to a certain extent been put in the picture, but it was often difficult not to stumble on some sensitive topic.

Fanny and Marcel, too, enjoyed the party, though I noted that Fanny's eyes never once left her husband: wherever he was in the crowded room, she would somehow manage to turn herself in his direction, occasionally flashing him a warning glance if his conversation with any of the women present became at all lively. Then she would break off her own conversation, make straight for him and demand attention: food or drink had to be fetched. It was, after all, her one night off. They had closed both bar and restaurant for that evening and she was not going to have her fun spoiled. Her red hair had been specially done for the occasion and the stray wisps that we usually saw peeping out from under her white cotton cap had been spray-fixed into total submission. The newly sleek head and unfamiliar thigh-hugging black dress with its plunging neckline was new to all of us, more in the style, it crossed my mind, of a smart Bordelaise than of our familiar Fanny.

It was only then that I realized how important Monsieur Pierre's fortnightly visit had become to her. His presence with Sylvie had transformed her life: he was her breath of fresh air, her sunshine. His courtesy and charm, the small attentions he paid her, just his presence was enough to compensate for the rough-hewn nature of her daily life. She did not seek any other life, but the leaven was there in Monsieur Pierre's and Sylvie's visits.

Sylvie could have been the daughter Fanny never had, and she would make up their bed with handsome linen sheets and embroidered pillowcases from her own trousseau, and put out perfumed soap and a small posy of flowers every other week-end in their secret room, as if perpetually decking the bridal bed. Marcel would have his little escapades: she could only try her utmost to foil his attempts. But Monsieur Pierre, now *he* would never behave like that. He was a gentleman, he was. Her customers would put their smelly feet, still with their boots on, on the top of the stove, so that she had to polish up the enamel every morning. Monsieur Pierre didn't do things like that, and in any case she was sure *his* feet didn't smell. *He* spoke to her with consideration and never tried to make a grab at her as she went by with a stack of dirty dishes. *He* would never attempt to put an arm round her waist, or make coarse jokes. He was her knight in shining armour. He kept the world sweet about her.

Then one Saturday night in June, it must have been at least ten years after their first visit, Monsieur Pierre asked Fanny and Marcel if they could spare half an hour in private with him and Sylvie. Fanny suddenly felt the world spin, as if someone had pulled a carpet out from beneath her feet. She knew from that moment that things would never be the same again.

When Monsieur Pierre spoke, his voice was steady and deliberate. He and Sylvie would never forget Fanny and Marcel and all the kindness they had shown them. 'But you see,' he explained, 'Sylvie is past thirty now and she has met a man who wants to marry her. She is very fond of him and I am sure they will be happy together. As you must realize, I cannot offer her that kind of security. To begin with, I'm too old, and in any case ... well, you know how it is ...' His voice trailed off wistfully. 'So we hope to make this a very special week-end, since it will, I am afraid, be our last. Marcel, what about some of your best champagne? Let's all share a bottle to start with, shall we?' So the four of them drank to Sylvie's happiness in her new life, while tears streamed down Fanny's face.

Now, almost another ten years on, Fanny still feeds the hungry hordes at lunch-time, and the occupants of the small tables in the evenings. Her food is still as good as ever, and she also makes pizzas to take away. The bar is still full of locals, and the stove still marked by their muddy boots in the winter. There is a pin-table too, now, to add to the jollity. But Fanny's temper has grown quicker and she slaps down anyone who dares attempt any

familiarity with her. Any woman entering the bar whom she thinks
might catch, or have once caught, Marcel's eye, is ostentatiously
cold-shouldered, and rumour has it that Marcel himself is not
infrequently subjected to what might perhaps be called 'proof of
the pudding' techniques, if ever Fanny guesses that more than his
eye might have strayed.

Newcomers to the bar might think that the place had always
been like that, but for those of us who knew it in the time of
Monsieur Pierre's visits, it is as if the heart had gone out of it. No
one ever mentions Monsieur Pierre or Sylvie, though I think that
Fanny must sometimes go away and have a good cry, all alone in
'their' room.

XII Two Weddings and a Swimming-pool

Three or four years after I had settled in France, Christine and William came to La Motte from England, on something of an impulse, and bought a 'fully restored fifteenth century cottage' in the village. For some time they had no longer felt at home in their English village, finding elderly retired colonels, maiden ladies of uncertain age and the local vicar poor company, and for a while had opted for the more rustic charms of the local pub. But then they decided that wine tasted better than beer and that the sun shone brighter in France, so there they were, determined to make the most of both these advantages.

They had gone for the 'fully restored fifteenth century cottage', since neither of them felt able to knock an old house into shape, the way most of us have done down here. And the house was pretty enough, even if it would have been hard, as in most of our houses, to identify any one item that actually dated from the fifteenth century, but the roof leaked badly and had to be re-done, and the garden turned out to be less than half the size they had been led to believe: in fact it soom became apparent that most of it actually belonged to the neighbouring property.

By then they already had a swimming-pool built where their somewhat unsuccessful lawn had been, and an occasional Lawson's Cypress did its uneasy best to screen it from the village street. It was not really the right property for them, but it would do, they thought.

Christine, who rapidly became known to her French acquaintances as Kiki, spent most of her days sunbathing, swimming and chatting to her neighbours (when they were not retired colonels or elderly maiden ladies). Our postman, who never did anything in a hurry, helped her improve her already excellent French, and learnt a little English, no doubt, in exchange; an arrangement that caused everyone's letters, on the days in question, to be delivered at about 3.30 in the afternoon, far too late for anyone to send a reply before the last collection. I'm sure she was never aware of this, and certainly meant no harm.

By the end of her first summer there, Kiki had become hazelnut-brown all over, and her auburn hair shone with golden lights where the sun had bleached it.

She planted some vegetables – just a few, beside the swimming-pool – but only until Annie and Raymond came to live in the little ruin next door, that Kiki had thought made such a romantic back-drop to her garden, and pointed out that her vegetable plot was actually on their land.

So Annie and Raymond put up a trellis-work fence, partly to delimit their garden, since Kiki seemed so vague about it all and William showed no interest in the matter at all, but especially to keep their two young children from straying, uninvited and unsupervised, into Kiki's pool.

Kiki objected to the fence and said it spoilt *her* view of *their* garden, which very soon became prettier than hers.

The only trouble with the trellis was that it didn't completely spoil Annie and Raymond's view of Kiki's garden, and it was sometimes quite hard to explain to guests, as they sat having drinks with them on the terrace, or barbecued sausages and chicken for Sunday lunch in the company of their children's school friends and their parents, who this glamorous naiad was who, regardless of neighbours, passing traffic and other onlookers, would step out of her house stark naked and walk the length of the garden to the pool, even stopping on the way to greet some passing acquaintance or hail the assembled diners next door through the trellis-work fence with a cheerful '*Bon appétit, Messieurs-Dames!*' She was very beautiful. She spoke excellent French. But one had to admit that it was a trifle disconcerting.

Things continued in this way for a couple of years during which the patchy hedge between pool and roadside gradually gave up trying to screen anything for want of effective co-operation. The pool was not in constant use: sometimes no one would go near it for days, then it would suddenly blaze into life, filled with squealing, splashing, writhing bodies, while the garden was littered with glasses, and music not necessarily to everyone's taste would blare from the terrace into the small hours of the morning.

Kiki had not thought about the weddings. She must have known they were to take place, since the mayor of a small village cannot marry two sons on two consecutive Saturdays without every one of the Commune's inhabitants knowing about it, and indeed, being invited to the Nuptial Mass and the *vin d'honneur* that follows.

It would, of course, have been much less trouble to have held the two weddings on the same Saturday, but the brides did not get on, so two separate occasions were planned: the younger son, now in his early twenties, was to marry his lifelong sweetheart on the first of July, and from that date take over his father's small farm, while the older boy, who had become a house painter and had already been living for three years with his *compagne*, was to consecrate the relationship on the eighth of the month.

The first wedding went according to plan. It was hot, but not so hot as to spoil things. But, since these occasions last all day and well into the night, by the time the second wedding took place, people had scarcely recovered from the first. And the temperature had risen sharply, so that when everyone awoke on the morning of the eighth, mouths were already parched after an unbearably hot night, and a heat haze trembled like a pale blue mist above even the coolest corners of the garden.

The beautiful old church was crowded: with every pew and chair filled, latecomers had to squeeze together on crumbling old benches, resting their backs against the church wall, craning their necks to see *les mariés*, and straining their ears to hear the proceedings, especially when Father Julio reached his homily, always a dangerously unpredictable moment when he officiated at funerals and marriages.

Struggling, like all our priests, to run about ten parishes instead of the one he had started with when he first arrived in this area from Italy in the early fifties, our priest does not receive unanimous support from all his parishioners. He is seen by many to have simply been here too long, not to understand the constraints of modern life, and to have, understandably perhaps, maintained closer connections with the numerous families who arrived, penniless for the most part, fleeing from Mussolini's Italy, than with the original Gascon families. Many parishioners prefer to go to mass in more distant parishes, feeling themselves out of harmony with the local incumbent. Others say 'better a bad priest

than none at all', and continue to support him. All of which leads
to much heart-searching for most of us. A pity.

On this particular occasion, even those who were accustomed to
his extraordinary sermons could hardly believe their ears when he
began to speak to the young couple. He elaborated for a while on
the sacramental and indissoluble nature of marriage. Then, feeling
that something more down-to-earth would be more readily
appreciated, he described marriage as the gift that each person
makes of himself to the other. This gift, he explained, was of
priceless value, and should be in all manner perfect. 'After all,' he
rambled on, his voice growing fainter until almost inaudible,
'After all, if you were to offer your best-beloved a bottle of
perfume, you would not give one that had been opened and used,
would you?' (Stifled gasps from the congregation.) 'Neither would
one like to discover that the set of chisels one had been given were
worn and blunted. What do you think?' he asked softly, wearing
the inscrutable smile of an elderly Cheshire cat.

It augured ill for the rest of the day. The bride's father, not
much of a church-goer at the best of times, was visibly angry, and
the mood during the rest of the mass was less reverent than usual.

Two trestle tables had been set up for the *vin d'honneur* on the
forecourt of the church in the middle of the village. Monsieur
Pochon from the village store opposite had, like everyone else,
accepted an invitation to the *vin d'honneur* after the wedding,
knowing that he could easily slip away to serve any customer who
might stop at his shop while he indulged in a free drink on the
opposite side of the road. There were dozens of bottles of white
wine, a handful of red and an occasional Pastis lurking in their
shadow, for those whose constitutions could not tolerate anything
as mild as wine. Transparent plastic mugs and a few baskets of
cheesy biscuits or bacon-flavoured crisps, known as *amuse-
gueules*, filled the rest of one table. The other was reserved for the
offerings brought by each guest, superbly gift-wrapped as always
by the shop at which they were purchased.

A hitch seemed to have occurred at this point, since the bride
had vanished, momentarily overcome with emotion perhaps, or
needing to fix a garter. However it was, her young husband was
left alone to welcome the guests and receive their good wishes as
he slowly but inexorably began to disappear under the mounting
pyramid of presents. Did he show slight traces of exasperation

when eventually his bride rejoined the party, or was it the slightly smug smile on his new sister-in-law's face that stirred a small black devil of revolt within him?

Far too much food and wine was consumed during the lunch that followed, at Fanny's, of course. But a wedding is a wedding, and everything must be done according to time-honoured custom. Traditional bawdy songs were sung and jokes told that made the younger women blush and suggest to their restless offspring that a bit of fresh air would do them no harm.

A brief pause around seven o'clock enabled those who had livestock needing attention at home, to weave their unsteady way back to cows, goats, hens or geese, while the newly-married couple raced around the countryside to visit all the old people who would have been present but for their infirmities.

This custom, known as *fleurir les Mémés*, used to consist of taking a posy of flowers to those too elderly to attend, in exchange for which a bottle of *vin vieux* was opened to toast the bride and groom. Nowadays the posy has become a white tulle rosette or bow, given to the old stay-at-home grannies, as well as to every guest before the ceremony, to adorn his lapel, and another for good measure to grace his car.

Another custom has likewise been transformed over the years: before beds were as we now know them, the bridal couch was thickly strewn with fresh green aromatic leaves, a form of rustic mattress, and none the worse for that. Now, the wedding attendants – young friends of bride and groom – spread green leaves, or even branches, at every cross-roads between the bride and groom's homes, the *Mairie* where they are to be married and the church that is to consecrate the civil union.

You will also often see a 'floral' archway, made of a single metal

hoop wound round with the same green branches and dotted with the ubiquitous tulle flowers, forming a gateway onto the road from a bride or groom's family home, through which they will pass on the wedding day, ceremonially escorted from their childhood haunts into the adult world of marriage with all its responsibilities and obligations.

Eventually the guests, still in their wedding finery in spite of the heat, which by now had become almost vicious, re-assembled at the village hall, where the mayor had organized supper and dancing for anyone who wished to join in the merriment.

Unfortunately, the village hall, referred to as '*la salle des fêtes*', was no ancient monument. It did no kind of justice to the pretty stone houses in the village, least of all to Kiki's 'fully restored fifteenth century cottage', which it faced across the narrow road from the far side of its roughly tarmacked car-park.

This lamentable structure had been voted for during the seventies by the all-male village council: eleven no doubt worthy but chauvinist peasant farmers, many of whom still to this day lack the most basic amenities in their homes for fear of putting up their rates. No sanitation (what's wrong with the cowshed anyway?); no bathroom (we've always managed at the kitchen sink, haven't we? So why waste money on pointless luxuries?) Naturally the hall was thought of in the same way: it should bring in money – dances, bingo (*quines*) and the occasional concert – (though here they had to admit that the church had the edge on the hall for that). Above all it had to be built cheaply.

The result was totally predictable: four walls, entirely unadorned save for two windows and a door, built of concrete blocks and rendered in steely-grey cement, and a roof of grey corrugated fibro-cement. What was wrong with that? It was all they needed, wasn't it? The walls kept the wind out, and the roof kept the rain off anyone who happened to be inside. Only not many people wanted to be inside. In the winter, only non-stop dancing could save its occupants from frostbite, while in the summer the hall became an inferno, even before one added the heat generated by human bodies.

And human bodies were not lacking on this last leg of the marathon. Music blared from the hall into the evening air, as guests struggled heroically with still more food and wine, attempting from time to time to shake it all down with a dance or two. Meanwhile the heat inside the building grew more and more intolerable as more and more guests piled in, determined not to miss any of the fun.

In the crush, the bridegroom lost sight of his bride. Perhaps she had been whirled off into the dancing throng, or maybe she had disappeared outside for a moment to cool off. He began to grow anxious, a sense of anxiety tinged with irritation. Why had she left him to cope this morning with all the guests and their presents? Could she not understand how embarrassing it had been for him? And now, whatever was she doing? Where was she? The intense heat, the wine and the emotions of the day were too much for him. He abandoned his guests and staggered to the door.

The sky still glowed pink from the sunset, bathing in an almost crimson light the village street, its old stone houses and, right opposite the hall, Kiki's swimming-pool. For a moment he thought the wine really had got the better of him, for there, standing along the edge of the pool that bordered the road was a whole row of girls, waggling their naked bottoms at him and shrieking with mirth.

For a split second he saw the fresco in the church, recently discovered under centuries of plaster, in which the naked bodies of the Damned are being pushed and prodded by a gleeful Devil into the steaming waters of a bubbling cauldron. Hell, it represented, so he had been told. Then someone called out: 'Come along in! Come and join us!'

Four strides took him across the road and through the remains of the hedge: he ripped off his clothes and leapt into the water.

After that things went from bad to worse. His father, appearing as if out of nowhere, begged him, first quietly, then in his customary roar, to return to his guests before his escapade was discovered by anyone else. His brother fetched a towel to cover him, but the bridegroom remained stubbornly in the water out of their reach. His new father-in-law was next on the scene, and there were words, followed by a scuffle between the two older men, while the bride stood by in floods of tears.

No one seemed able ever to give an authentic account of how it all ended. Ill-feeling between the two families was evidently short-lived, though, since a couple of months later they spent a day in Lourdes together.

As for Kiki, she put her 'fifteenth century cottage with swimming-pool' on the market, accusing Annie and Raymond of 'suburban mentalities' when they took down their trellis-work fence and built a six foot wall in its place.

XIII   The House that Jack Bought

Then there was Jack, who, although not French, any more than Kiki was, like her spoke very respectable French and was, at any rate in his earlier years here, very much part of our village. I used to meet him quite often at our weekly market: it wasn't a big market, but useful nevertheless. He was a gregarious chap, so one met him at other people's houses, where he was an excellent guest, and from time to time I would run into him, alone or in company at Fanny's where he would eat fairly frequently in his more prosperous days. He really was a rather extraordinary character, and, like most of us, I suppose, grew increasingly quirky as he grew older. Not an altogether easy man to get on with, many would tell you, though I can honestly say that I, for my part, never saw that side of him.

No one around here seemed to know how Jack had made his money when he lived in England, and indeed there was not much of it left by the time he reached his eighties. He did own his house, and a small amount of rather fine antique furniture, mostly English oak, and a splendid eighteenth-century brass doorstop, which was to disappear mysteriously after his death.

He had been one of the early settlers in this peaceful corner of France, having, like so many of us, been enticed by one of those 'Oh-so-tempting' advertisements that used to appear weekly in the up-market Sunday press, inviting us to come and look at delightful, though abandoned, farm buildings, *maisons de maître*, or even small châteaux, with a view to acquiring a cheap holiday house, or indeed, as Jack had done, settling here permanently after retirement.

In those days – I'm talking about the sixties and early seventies –

the local French peasants (the name they give themselves, but woe betide anyone calling them that to their faces, for they would regard it as an insult) had grown weary of their ancient farmhouses with their crumbling stone and damp floors, and were busily dotting their fields with small, rather ugly, rendered brick bungalows, only to have to admit that these were less well protected from the burning summer sun and a lot more cramped than the old houses they had come to despise.

So it was that anyone with the necessary time, energy, imagination and a modicum of money to restore one of these cast-off dwellings could find himself the enchanted owner of a splendidly spacious stone residence, with enough old beams, elegant fireplaces and quaint nooks and crannies to make any English suburban heart almost burst with excitement and pride.

Jack had bought a large house with magnificent views over gently rolling vine-covered hills, about three kilometres on the other side of la Motte from me, a far more splendid place than he could ever have obtained in Britain. A second, smaller house stood behind the main house, lurking, as it were, in its shadow, but as it seemed to be part of the deal, he reckoned that something could be done with it, even if it wasn't a patch on the 'big house'.

Then there was an orchard, and an acre or so of grass. And he wasn't that young. Nor very energetic either, preferring to sit and admire 'his' view, preferably with a glass of white wine in his hand.

So the summers slipped by, the wine enhanced the view, and not much was done to modernize the house. He did manage to grow a few vegetables, which largely kept him going, and he ate out with friends whenever he was invited. He was a very popular guest: he always arrived on time, looking smart and impeccably clean as if about to face a sergeant-major. He even wore a tie, an item that most of us have conveniently forgotten about since coming to live here, and he had a fund of good stories, just gossipy enough to be innocently amusing without making the listener feel guilty of trespass.

Thinking about our encounters afterwards, I found myself marvelling at the sheer amount of information he seemed to have stored in his memory about everything and everyone. His piercing eyes missed nothing and his total recall was prodigious. What if he were ever tempted to write his memoirs, even thinly disguised as a novel, what mayhem he could cause amongst his many acquaintances!

But it seemed that he just loved sitting and admiring his view. Even in the winter he would settle in a sheltered corner with a glass of wine at his elbow, until the chilly sunset air drove him indoors to light a small fire and pour himself a whisky. He read quite a lot, watched the French news, and not much more, on television, wrote a few letters to his three children and an occasional one to *The Times*.

Jack's closest friends were the Allenbys, who had known him when he still lived in England. He had been their neighbour in Kenilworth for a number of years, and although Peter Allenby once remarked that Jack had always been 'a bit of a rogue', he and Janice were very attached to the old boy, as they referred to him, and did a great deal to help him. Eventually they themselves bought a place down here quite close to Jack's, and would spend whatever time there that they could manage, relaxing from the pressures of business and keeping a weather eye on their friend. Jack's pension never seemed to stretch quite far enough, so in addition to giving practical assistance about his house, Peter would often make him a small allowance to help out. And of course the wine store was always replenished before the Allenbys went back, as was the supply of logs for the winter. It occurred to me that they were more like a son and daughter to Jack than his own children, who rarely set foot in the place.

One evening he was eating out, as I was too, invited by the Allenbys to one of the best restaurants in the area. The *nouvelle cuisine*, I am glad to say, had passed this excellent place by, and a meal at the 'Beau Regard' was still a meal. Here a *magret* is a *magret*: an entire breast of duck, lightly roasted, cut into parallel, wafer-thin slices, so that it holds it shape on the plate, served with appropriate vegetables and a rich, succulent sauce. Sauces, *light*, of course, are served with the *nouvelle cuisine* too, but wash about the plate among the five slices of cucumber and twin mini new potatoes, having neither the consistency to cover anything, nor indeed anything to cover beyond a finger of turbot or three slivers of partridge. Although I deplore meals so huge and excessive that one cannot face food for days afterwards, I shall never be convinced that making a piece of cucumber look like a water-lily has anything whatever to do with cooking.

Be that as it may, Jack did honour to his hosts that evening. Ageing and rather gaunt, when dressed to dine out he suddenly appeared rejuvenated: straight-backed and stiff in a spotless shirt, well-creased trousers, his shoes, handmade many decades ago, resplendent with years of polishing, he became the life and soul of the proceedings. He ate and drank more than anyone else, his eyes sparkling with malicious delight while he fed the other members of the party delicate titbits of information about this person and that; when eventually the final coffee with its accompanying *digestif* had been taken, he would bid all a good night and weave his somewhat unsteady way home in his red Mini, while the rest of us crossed our fingers and prayed to the Almighty to keep the local French off the roads that Jack would be using.

Then one day, feeling the pinch a bit more than usual, Jack had an idea: 'If I were to sell my house,' he beamed, delighted at the scheme he had just thought up, 'If I sold my house – the big one, I mean – I could move into the smaller one and have enough money to live on comfortably for years!' It did indeed seem a good idea and very soon he had found a buyer and a deal was done. Jack sold the large house with the land that lay in front of it, and enough land behind to allow comfortable access. He retained for his own use the smaller house with its narrow front garden, and the field that lay beyond the two houses, which had a kind of concrete shed on it large enough for a combined garage and workshop.

There were problems with the new neighbour from the outset. She, understandably, wanted to be left alone to get on with her own life. Jack, in an effort to be 'helpful', offered the loan of various household wares until such time as Maria could get her own stuff shipped over. Unfortunately, Maria clearly did not think much of Jack's three battered aluminium saucepans, nor of the dour and none too clean ex-army blankets offered; when the saucepans were in due course returned, Jack said they must have been used for anything but cooking, since he was convinced they were even more dented than when he had last seen them. And as for the blankets, his fury knew no bounds: Maria had used them, he claimed, not as blankets, but as *rugs*, strewn over the old tiled floors for people to *walk* on!

'But how can you possibly be sure of that, Jack?' Peter asked him when all this trouble blew up.

'Don't imagine I don't know what goes on there,' Jack replied with a knowing curl to his upper lip. 'Don't forget I've got those very powerful binoculars, and if you think I can't tell they're my blankets on the floors....' His face was purple with outrage and Peter had quite a job to calm him down.

After a few months of similar incidents, Jack was heard to declare: 'Anyone who is a friend of hers is no friend of mine!' And that, where Jack was concerned, was that.

There followed a year or so largely taken up with legal disputes concerning some boundary problem, and by the time all this had been sorted out, and Jack had been obliged at his own expense to convene the *Géomètre* to re-define the boundaries between them, his relationship (if such it could be called) with Maria had reached a point of no return, since his hatred of her seemed absolute. Not only did he feel years older, but his resources were further diminished by legal fees and bills from the *Géomètre*. Something had to be done.

'I know the house I'm in now is nothing like as big as the other,' Jack said to Peter and Janice one evening when they had come over, freshly arrived from England, to see how he was. They were sitting together on the front porch of the smaller house, looking down on the back of his original home, now inhabited by his arch-enemy. It was indeed true, Janice noted, that almost everything that went on there could be seen from where they sat. And if you added powerful binoculars.... At one stage of her life she would not have believed that Jack, or anyone else among her friends, would do a thing like that – pry into someone else's life to that extent, she meant. But now she was not so sure, and the realization brought an unwelcome sense of foreboding.

But Jack was busy explaining his new scheme: he would convert the 'garage' into a house – 'quite big enough for my needs, you know, and by selling this house as well, I'll be in the clear for what remains of my life. And in any case, when it's all gone, and I've nothing left to live on, I'll take the hint.... Don't believe in hanging around beyond a certain point, you know. Wrote for the little booklet the Euthanasia Society advertises; it came the other day. Useful to have by one; you never know.'

'Oh Jack, I hope you'll always remember to ask us when there is anything special you need. We can't always guess, and as you know, we aren't here all the time, but you know, you only have to ask and we'll help if we possibly can.' Peter noted a glint in Jack's eye. No, he wasn't going dotty, Jack was very much still all there.

'So what's been going on here this winter?' asked Peter, hoping not so much to receive choice morsels of local gossip as to distract Jack and steer the conversation onto more cheerful topics.

'Ah, here indeed! No, I don't suppose you would have heard

this one, although everyone else seems to be *au courant*. Though I am the one to know what really goes on across the way, don't you think? A passionate affair, I think it used to be called. A passionate affair, and with all the trappings, believe me. Quite entertaining sometimes.' And Jack gave a sudden roar, a mixture of mirth and cynical exuberance that made Peter and Janice jump. Definitely, the old chap was not dotty, but he was different. Different in an indefinable way.

In due course the concrete 'garage' became Jack's home. A wall was built roughly across the middle, to divide the bedroom from the living room, a tiny corner of which was screened off as a kitchen, while one wall of the bedroom housed a shower, a washbasin and a WC in part of a long cupboard, the rest of which was reserved for storage. A large deep green enamelled stove in the living-room kept the whole place warm in the winter, and the general effect was pleasing, for the best pieces of furniture had been reserved for this room, and a few good pictures and silver-framed photographs of his children, not forgetting the brass doorstop, gave one a feeling of cossetted comfort. And when summer came, there was the small garden to tend, a few lettuces, carrots and radishes to grow, and always his favourite white wine to sip as he sat in a deck chair admiring the sunset.

And it wasn't only the sunset that he could see from his terrace, for now he could overlook not only Maria and her friend, whom Jack insisted on referring to as her '*amoureux*', whenever he came to visit her, but also the new people who had bought his second house, who, it had to be admitted, were not at all interesting in that way, but who no doubt would turn out to have a few intriguing quirks for him to allow his mind to dwell on. And as his living-room window offered more or less the same view as the terrace, he did not have to confine his surveillance of his neighbours to the summer months, but could speculate on and confirm theories about their lives and activities the whole year round, an occupation that gave him increasing pleasure, especially as it was beginning to point a way to getting his own back on Maria for the wrongs he was convinced she had done him.

Let it be said that Jack was sufficiently discreet not to draw undue attention to what he was doing. He pottered in his garden, he sat on the terrace, book in hand and a glass at his elbow, and could well have been watching birds with his ever-present binoculars. In fact, he was a keen bird-watcher, an interest he shared with the new neighbours, who had lived near the sea before and were knowledgeable about sea-birds, but less so about the garden and inland varieties, of whom a certain number managed to escape the most sinister of their predators, the local *chasseurs*, for whom anything that moves or flies is worth shooting, even if the odd song-thrush does not make much of a meal.

So they would talk with Jack about his *Dame Blanche*, the barn-owl who spewed out blackened pellets the size of a small hen's egg, containing the recognizable indigestible remnants of her nocturnal feast of mice; they would admire the great buzzards, *les buses*, who described huge circles around his house each day when the sun was at its zenith, their wings motionless as they rose higher and still higher in an accommodating thermal, their pleasure in this effortless flight expressed in a thin, ethereal mewing.

'I don't know about you, Jack,' said Elsa, his new neighbour, as she and her husband sat on Jack's terrace one evening. 'I don't know how you feel, but I hate these hunters who invade our fields and gardens and frighten off all the birds, even if they don't manage to kill them all. What do you think?'

'Oh, I entirely agree. Won't have them near the place if I can help it. Though it's sometimes hard to stand up in front of a man holding a gun and tell him to get the hell out of here. I don't believe in keeping guns around, anyway. Too many accidents.'

'Actually, we do have a gun in the house, though it's not one of those hunting guns, is it, Paul?' Elsa added, turning to her husband.

'No, I had a licence to carry a pistol – to do with my job, you know – and I brought the thing out here. You never know, living in a rather isolated place like this. Actually, the local police recommend one to keep either a large dog or a gun and I reckon a gun doesn't cost as much to feed!'

'Well, that's one way of looking at it,' Jack replied with a great guffaw. 'I suppose I'm lucky not to have any possessions left worth taking. Even my wine cellar isn't what it used to be. It all has to be bought on an *ad hoc* basis now. No money, you know. And nowhere to store the stuff if I had!'

Later on, after Paul and Elsa had walked back to their house and Jack had made himself an omelette, as he washed his plate, the three glasses, and wiped the omelette pan with a piece of kitchen paper (one of his children had taught him that trick, after the divorce, when he had to learn to cook for the first time,) he noticed that he only had three bottles of wine left, plus a remnant of whisky, which he proceeded to pour himself. Something had to be done; he needed wine the way most people need wholesome food to keep healthy: for him it was a necessity. As he sat sipping his whisky he had an idea. Then another. And another. Ideas tumbled over one another until they spilled over like water from an overfilled flower vase: once the process has started, there is no way of stopping the entire contents from siphoning out onto the table. He had been worried about his future for too long. Something had to give, he thought, as the ideas gushed forth into his consciousness and he struggled to restore some order to the chaos in his head.

The following day, observing that Maria was alone in her house, Jack put on his best shoes, trousers, shirt, jacket and tie and paid her a visit. Since the last time they had spoken (and acrimoniously at that,) must have been at least three years back, Maria showed no small amazement at this new development.

'Well, now ... I hardly expected a visit from you, and this morning of all times. What do you want?' she asked somewhat abruptly, wishing that Jos had been around, and not on his way up into the Dordogne for a couple of days.

'As a matter of fact, I've come to ask you and Jos if you will do me a small service. It shouldn't cause you much trouble. You see,' he went straight to the point, 'You see, I need someone to keep me supplied fairly regularly with that nice white wine Monsieur Briand makes over in Saint-Sulpice,' he waved vaguely in the direction of a neighbouring hamlet, 'and with an occasional bottle of whisky – once a week would probably be enough, though that could be arranged as necessary....'

Maria's face had gone a deep beetroot red as if she were about to burst with rage. But she was no fool, and realized some, if not all, of the implications of this brazen approach. Jack stood impassive, allowing his words to sink in, the merest trace of a smile on his lips, while his eyes remained steely and obdurate.

'And supposing I say not on your nelly?' Maria ventured, though the words carried more conviction than the manner in which they were spoken. 'Supposing I were to tell you to get out of my house – yes, my house – and go back to your ... garage, or whatever you care to call it?'

Now it has never been revealed exactly how Jack persuaded Maria to agree to his request, though it must be assumed he left no stone unturned in order to induce her to see things his way. Then, having said what he had come to say, he gave a stiff little bow, turned sharply on his heel, went out through the door and straight home, noting as he crossed the grass between the two houses that Elsa and Paul were still not back from their weekly shopping expedition to the nearest supermarket. He had not miscalculated his manoeuvre.

So, apparently miraculously, what had appeared to be a lifelong feud suddenly took on the complexion of a cosy weekly visit, and Jack's 'supplies' were kept topped up at no cost to himself. And yet, in spite of assistance from Peter and Janice Allenby, he never seemed to have enough money to get by. His children would write and ask for help with this and that: and how could he, their father, not respond? So Jack would send them something.

Isolated from others as they were, Jack's three houses, as he still liked to think of them, offered complete seclusion from prying eyes, except, of course, from those of their inhabitants. He had therefore arranged that the weekly visit from Maria and Jos should always take place when Paul and Elsa were out, or under cover of darkness during the winter months. Given the fact that the nearest supermarket, where they did their main shopping, was twenty minutes' drive away, unless something really untoward happened, once they had left their house they could be counted on to be away for some considerable time. So no one ever got to know about the visits, and Jack saw how well his idea was working out. Pity he had not thought of it sooner, he sometimes said to himself. To his friends he continued to refer to Maria in his usual derogatory manner, while remaining more or less discreet about her in other ways.

One winter evening, when his binoculars could offer him no joy, Jack began to give more serious consideration to another idea that had burgeoned during the Allenbys' last visit. They were spending so much money, or so he considered, on restoring their old house, that they surely must be better off than they implied to him. Of course, he could only make jokes about it: being an English gentleman he could not actually ask them about their financial position the way a Frenchman might well have done, but he suspected more money than they admitted to. Yes, yes, they gave him a small hand-out from time to time, and very nice too, but surely.... Well, it deserved careful thought, and a good glass of Maria's whisky to lubricate the wheels and cogs of his ageing brain.

Jack was indeed ageing: he found it increasingly difficult to

summon the energy to get into his little car and drive to the village.
So he got the baker to deliver his bread three times a week. It cost
a bit more, but who cared? He had someone in once a week to tidy
the place up – rather a thankless task, since it was all beginning to
look very scruffy and really needed a major spring-clean. But in
spite of the slow deterioration of his physical state, and the
dilapidation of his surroundings, his mind remained as needle-
sharp and cogent as ever, or at least, so it seemed to the casual
observer and, even more important, to him, since his recent ideas
could not be discussed with anyone, but had to be worked out
entirely alone.

When the spring came and his cherry tree was full of buds, he
strolled over to see his other neighbour, Paul.

'Ah! Paul. Good to see you on this lovely sunny morning. I
wondered if I could have a quiet word with you. Would it be
convenient now, or would you prefer some other time?'

'No, it's perfectly convenient now, actually. Come into my little
study; we'll be quite on our own there. Elsa is busy with something
or other in the garden, planting out some of her seedlings, I think.
It's her great passion, that garden.' A passion that Jack was well
aware of. He had, of course, chosen his moment to approach Paul;
seeing Elsa on hands and knees in a flower bed, he thought she
would be unlikely to join them within the time he needed to make
his request to Paul.

'I remember you and Elsa mentioning once that you had a
pistol. I've got a bit of a problem with some creature that's lurking
around my house at night, and I'm frightened that if I don't get rid
of it, it could get in under the roof tiles. You know what these
things are. A marten I think, very deft and slinky, but once they
get in, you're really in trouble. So if I could possibly borrow your
pistol for a few days I thought I might be able to, well . . . let's say,
discourage it, don't you know . . .

Paul was dumbfounded. For a start, a pistol was not a suitable
weapon for killing martens or other predators, for that matter.
And even more important, it was his pistol, registered in his name,
and simply could not be lent to anyone else. He was surprised at
old Jack asking such a thing. Besides, Jack's insistence, and that
glint in his eye, it made him feel more than a little uncomfortable.
He had always tried to keep out of Jack's life, while remaining a
good neighbour, for he sensed that trouble lay in that direction.
He and Elsa had remained friendly but kept their distance. Now

he was being drawn into something he sensed was not quite what it seemed.

'I'm sorry about the marten, Jack, but I think we'll have to find some other way of getting rid of it. You see, I simply cannot lend my pistol to anyone, for whatever reason. I'm sure you'll understand; the licence is in my name, and that makes me responsible. Sorry. Now, what can we find out about martens? You do have reason to think that that's what it is, do you? I believe the locals poison them with specially treated eggs. I'll try to find out more and let you know.'

But Jack seemed to have lost interest in the matter, mumbled an excuse about expecting a phone call, and made his way back to his own house empty-handed.

Shortly afterwards Paul and Elsa began to look for another house. They wanted a change, they said to close friends, but did not want the matter generally known. Had they become aware of the regular visits Maria and Jos made to Jack, in spite of all his precautions? His attempt to borrow the pistol had certainly upset them. Did they think he was becoming bizarre in his old age, and that they would be happier further away from him and his problems? However it was, they found a convenient house near a village but not adjacent to other houses, and, without waiting to sell the house next to Jack's, moved away, lock, stock and barrel.

Jack made a couple of visits to the nearest large town; a long trip that took him the best part of a day, what with the necessary research into the discreet acquisition of a gun. But Jack was tenacious if nothing else, and once a plan had been conceived, he would persist until its last detail was carried out to his satisfaction, leaving nothing to chance, and no room for error. His schemes had worked admirably so far, and he had no doubts that they would continue to do so, provided proper attention was paid to detail. Detail. Every detail. That was what he thought of as he sat in his chair by the window, looking out over the early summer landscape, sipping Maria's ever-generous supply of whisky. Remarkable how almost friendly they were, Maria and Jos, when they brought his supplies each week. They even did the odd bit of shopping for him when he felt he needed a little more help, and would bring things he had ordered by phone from the chemist. He would, of course, pay them for these extras: they were not part of the original understanding, and he did know how to keep his side of a bargain. After all, he was a gentleman and a man of honour.

When the Allenbys arrived one evening in June, as planned, Peter rang Jack and arranged to go round on the afternoon of the following day, after they had settled themselves in. But as Janice still had things to do in the house – it had been empty all winter and needed a thorough clean – Peter went off by himself to see his old friend.

Janice had just finished her cleaning and had prepared a cup of tea, when Peter appeared, trembling uncontrollably, ashen-faced and visibly terrified.

'For heaven's sake, Peter, whatever has happened?' Never in their long life together had she seen him like this. 'What's the matter? Is it Jack? For goodness' sake *say* something!'

It took Peter quite a while before he could speak, and then the words came haltingly, almost in a whisper, as if he could not believe what he himself was saying, so monstrous did it seem.

'When I got to Jack's, he asked me in as usual, but I noticed he locked the door on the inside and pocketed the key. I was puzzled, naturally, and made a joke about it. "Frightened I might rush away too soon, eh! Jack? Don't worry, I've got all afternoon. We can have a good long chat." But I noticed his eyes, and when he told me abruptly to sit down at his desk, I really did begin to wonder what was going on. He was on the far side of the desk, and you probably remember there is a drawer on that side too. Well, he took a ruddy pistol out of the drawer and pointed it straight at me.'

'No!' exclaimed Janice, 'Not a real one, it couldn't have been a real one. Where would he have got one? He must have meant it as a joke ...' Her voice trailed off as Peter broke in:

'Janice, I assure you the gun was real, *and* loaded, *and* cocked. That's the trouble, no one is going to believe what I say. At least you, you must hear me out. He wanted money, lots of money. He told me to write him a cheque for ten thousand pounds then and there. I told him that I didn't keep that sort of money in my current account and that the cheque would bounce, but he had it all worked out. "Well in that case," he said, "just write me an IOU for ten thou and instruct your bank tonight to make the necessary arrangements to honour it. Perfectly simple, you see. But I want that money, and I know you can afford it. So let's have no fuss, shall we?"

'I couldn't believe what was happening, Janice. Our friend Jack. It was a nightmare. But he brought the gun closer and closer across the desk and I had visions of his tripping and the thing going off – it was perfectly ghastly, a kind of horror-picture in slow motion. So I wrote out the IOU and asked whether I could go home. I could hardly drive because I had begun to tremble and shake all over....'

'What do we do now?' asked Janice. 'Supposing he comes round here? If he's off his nut, as he must be, then we ought to make ourselves scarce. Perhaps we have just been fools and not seen it all coming. Either way, we can't stay here, I reckon.

'Yes, you're right. I've been too shattered to think of what the next step should be, but the sooner we pack up and go back to England the better, you're quite right. I thought of getting the police, but with my rudimentary French and the improbability of the whole thing, I don't know where that would get us. So let's pack as soon as possible and get off. Oh, dear, I feel quite sick with the shock of it all.'

Janice rang her various friends who, knowing they had arrived, would be expecting to see them. Keeping her voice as steady as she could, she told them that something had cropped up at home, something to do with Peter's work and that she was ever so sorry but they were having to go back. And go back they did, leaving before dawn, having spent the night loading the car once again and shutting up the house. When they lay down to try to snatch an hour's sleep, they were unable to stop talking about what had happened. It was indeed like a nightmare: they could hardly believe it, yet knew it was true, and the conflict between plausibility and fact grew deeper as they attempted to understand why their old friend had done this terrible thing and what sort of a person he really was.

By the time they reached Cherbourg after what seemed like an eternity of driving, they had decided that all they could do, and should do, was to contact their local police on arrival home and ask their advice.

They slept a little on the ferry, from sheer exhaustion, and heard nothing of the usual information about landing cards, passports, the bureau de change or the duty free opening hours. Neither were they troubled by the tramping footsteps and shouts of 'Here we are!' from latecomers to their cabins, who had preferred to dine in the restaurant or drink at the bar before retiring for what remained of the night. They just slept for the few allotted hours, and woke to the sharp rap of the steward on their cabin door, announcing as he passed along the narrow corridor that breakfast was being served and that they must be ready for disembarkation in three quarters of an hour.

They were on the road by seven and headed north through the rain, that seemed to have set in for the day.

The police in Kenilworth could not have been more helpful. They did say, however, that as far as the French side of things was concerned, this was a matter for Interpol. Clearly something had to be done, or the Allenbys would never feel safe to return to their French house. And yet Janice and Peter did not want to harm their old friend; but what else could they do? They spent the summer miserably at home in England: they could not find out anything about what was happening to Jack, as they felt they had to keep the whole matter secret and could hardly contact him directly.

In due course two French police inspectors, delegated by Interpol, went to see Jack. They were there for three hours and took away the pistol and some scribbled notes.

Five days later Jack was found dead in the chair beside the window of his living-room, an empty whisky bottle and an empty glass beside him on the small table. On his desk, a foot or so away, there was an equally empty bottle labelled 'Paracetamol', and the binoculars.

The glass showed traces of paracetamol. And so did the bottle. It seemed as if old Jack had done the thing properly. And since the Allenbys, who had alerted Interpol, were still in England, and no one else was known to be in the habit of visiting Jack, except his weekly 'help', who had discovered him, '*raide-mort dans son fauteuil favori*' ('stone dead in his favourite chair', as she put it) and as his door was never locked, it seemed futile to look any further. At his age, it could even have been natural causes.

None of his children attended the funeral, though someone subsequently broke into the abandoned house and took away most of his possessions. No one seemed to know what had happened to the brass doorstop, and the ensuing feud over that and the furniture prevented the house being sold, as they could not agree on a valuation.

Nature has done the rest: a Russian Vine has got in through the broken windows, the walls show fissures where you can still see them under brambles, the door won't close any more, winter frosts have wrecked the plumbing, and the roof leaks. The Allenbys visit their own house again, I'm glad to say, since they are good friends of mine, but they won't go anywhere near Jack's old place. And I must say I don't blame them.

Of course the vast majority of British people here live quiet lives, untroubled by anything more tiresome than the vagaries of local and national administration, and waiting for the builder or electrician. Too much has already been written by others about that aspect of life in France for me to elaborate on such matters here, and indeed I sometimes wonder whether the British do not suffer some of the same trials back in their own country, even if in not so Gallic a form.

But it is a fact that in quite a few Communes in this area the British form a sizeable slice of the population, and are on the whole well regarded by the local people, who boast to one another of '*nos Anglais*', meaning the family to whom they have sold an old house, and with whom they often form pretty close ties. It was a pity for Jack, in a way, especially as he spoke very creditable French, that he was never lucky enough to form such ties with a French farming family, who might have helped to make his last years less troubled, who knows? But perhaps he preferred things that way.

XIV Fernando

La Motte, being a fairly large village, had a number of features not found in all the villages around here. For a start it had two cafés: 'Chez Fanny', our restaurant, and the 'Café de la Halle', on one corner of the market square, with a lively bar and a warm welcome from Henriette and Victor, the couple who ran it. We had our church, our chemist, our doctor, our post office, the two shops and a school. And of course, we also had Fernando, who lived in the village, but whose land adjoined that of the Boniface family. Now Fernando was a popular man, helpful to anyone who needed help, and above all good humoured and ready for a laugh and what he always referred to as 'A bit of fun'. He lived on the edge of the village, near the *Halle*, or covered market square, although his land and farm buildings lay between the Boniface farm, my house, and the main road leading north from the village, where the old forge was.

Fernando worked his land more or less unaided; he had twelve cows and a bull called Tino, some vines from which he made wine for the family, with some over for sale, and some plum trees. He grew a little wheat, alternating with oats, and some maize down at the end of his land, on the hill that led up to the edge of my garden. And of course there were the hens, ducks and turkeys, along with a large vegetable plot that kept the whole family fed throughout the year. He was not overworked, and the restricted size of his land – ten hectares of his own, and five rented, largely for the cows – made it possible for him to take time off, more or less whenever he felt like it, to do a bit of hunting. And when I say hunting I don't mean only birds and beasts – he did that too – but one must perforce include anything in skirts within range, since his passion for the female of his species seemed to be insatiable. Poor Thérèse knew all about that, I suspect, though I do not think in the event that it was that that did her much harm.

Most of the women in the surrounding countryside were married and worked on their farms with their husbands, which did not make it easier for Fernando to get close to them, although he was a man who would spot and seize the most slender of opportunities. Then there were a few widows, and of course young girls growing up. But when Helen came to live in an ancient cottage not far from Fernando's old farmhouse, and he saw that she seemed independent and to all intents and purposes unattached, he did his utmost to be helpful and charming.

Anyway, one day not very long ago something dramatic happened in the village.

Fernando would normally be up and about only by seven, now he had got rid of the cows and there was less to do on the farm, but that morning someone ran shouting up the steps to his front door a few minutes before six and hammered on the oak, clamouring incoherently.

Fernando was awake and had pulled on his clothes in a flash. No one would dare to rouse him for a joke, so there must be something wrong. Perhaps his neighbour's cows had got into his fields. Or an accident. Perhaps one of his brothers ... or one of the girls, or maybe their children. Heaven forbid that anything should happen to his little grandchildren! Perhaps the old people ... The telephone was useful enough, but he still preferred the old ways of carrying good or bad tidings: by word of mouth. Whatever was wrong, at least someone had taken the trouble to come.

It was André, the village carpenter. He was always the first now in the square of a morning. Henriette from the Café on the corner didn't really open at that hour, but she never refused young André his early morning coffee, however bleary-eyed she felt, and when Fernando saw him standing there at the top of the steps, hopping in agitation from one foot to the other and wringing his hands as he glanced back over his shoulder along the narrow street that led to the *Halle*, he was not at all prepared for what he saw.

For there, in the corner of the covered market, where for years now he had always left his precious shiny blue motorbike in complete safety, was a small pile of charred metal, twisted in an agony of heat, consumed almost to dust, unrecognizable and irrecuperable ashes.

Breakfast was a gloomy meal. Not that he spoke much at

mealtimes anyway. Now the girls were all gone from home, he and Madeleine had little more than platitudes to exchange. And he didn't want any questions about the bike: there were so many possibilities. But can you imagine anyone doing something like that just because his wife or his daughter had had a bit of fun? People were extraordinary, he thought. After all, it was only fun. Not as if he wanted anything more than just that, was it?

'What are you going to do?' asked Madeleine, her hands still trembling as she poured his coffee.

'Do? What do you expect me to do? Ride away on the thing?'

'I mean, are you going to tell the gendarmerie?'

'And what do you imagine they can do about it? Buy me a new one, perhaps?' he went on scathingly. Like a hurt child, he hit out at anyone who tried to console him. He did not want to be consoled. He wanted his beautiful shiny blue motorbike back.

He got up and went out. The six shallow steps from the front door swept down in a graceful curve to the level of the road, then continued on in a kind of double spiral to a semi-basement in which the family kept their weekly supply of potatoes, some of their winter carrots, and other perishables. A little wine was stored here, too, though the bulk of what was made each year remained at the farm, about a kilometre outside the village. He had a workshop down here in the basement, and here he kept his push-bike, which he used every day to go to work on the farm.

People often asked why Madeleine and he lived where they did, when they had animals to care for at the farm, but Fernando would always reply that Madeleine preferred living in the village, because it was less lonely for her. I suspect that it also meant much greater freedom for him.

'How I wish I had been a secretary, or a typist,' Madeleine told me once. 'Anything rather than a farmer's wife! I hate the country: all the mud in the winter, and the heat in the summer. And the awful hard work, day in and day out. It's bad enough in the village, but down there, ugh!'

Actually, living in the village as she did, she would do her housework in the mornings, make lunch for the two of them, then, after washing the dishes and tidying up, she would walk down to the farm, collect what was needed for their next meals from the freezer and the vegetable plot, then pass the time of day with her old parents. They had not wanted to leave the land, and lived on alone in the two-roomed cottage opposite the old farmhouse itself, which now stood empty and forlorn, its main room containing nothing but a huge freezer, into which went the hens, ducks, rabbits, turkeys, pork and veal that the farm produced, carefully wrapped and labelled to see them all through the winter.

It was true that her life was arduous at certain times of the year: she had to help with hay-making and bringing in the straw; she helped to plant their tomatoes and gathered them, along with the beans, salads, onions, carrots, peppers, aubergines, courgettes and artichokes.

When the time came to pick the grapes, she, along with all their friends and relations, which included me on many an occasion, would snip away all morning at the heavy bunches with the traditional tiny secateurs, emptying her trug whenever it was full into the *hotte*, which Fernando her husband carried around strapped to his back, to be tipped up periodically over the high-sided trailer before it became too heavy to manage. To empty the *hotte* satisfactorily you have to climb a short ladder propped against one side of the trailer, and when you consider yourself to be high enough, you bend double in a single, sharp movement, thus pouring the grapes out over your head into the trailer. If you don't double up enough or do so too slowly, you end up with the grapes in your hair and round your ears! It is quite a tricky operation and requires a man of considerable strength.

On these occasions Madeleine would stop picking at about half past eleven in order to help her old mother finish the preparations for the special *vendange* lunch, during which we ate and drank copiously and well, with much laughter and joking, before resuming our work, which often continued until sundown. They were exhausting days, but fun.

At the appropriate season she and her mother would kill and prepare the poultry and rabbits, though her husband always fed them and saw that they were safely locked up at night. But Fernando never asked her to drive the tractor, nor would she have anything to do with the twelve cows, the bull (Tino), the calves, or Fernando's dog. In fact, going to live in the village house had been quite a shrewd move on her part, and most days she managed her time very much as she wanted to.

Of course, Madeleine was rather frail, so it was said, though most people suspected she was tougher than she appeared to be. She had had a mysterious breakdown many years before, but exactly what it had all been about, no one seemed to be clear. It was then that the family had come to live in the village house: an elegant, long building that had once been, of all things, a convent. Certain people in the village laughed at the incongruity of Fernando living in a convent, and some spoke of the nuns turning in their graves. He was a law unto himself, was Fernando.

Before coming back up the lower flight of stone steps with his bicycle, Fernando took out his pocket knife and pruned back a particularly vigorous branch of one of his *Etoile de Hollande* that rampaged over the house, smothering the lower floor with heavily-perfumed deep red roses, and forever trying to insinuate themselves into the upper floor windows whenever he was not looking. Helen, who lived in a tiny cottage not far from the one occupied by Fernando's parents-in-law, had given him a couple of well-rooted cuttings twelve or more years back, it must be by now, he thought, and they had prospered and were much admired.

When Helen had shut the door in his face, he had wanted to tear out the red roses in fury and pique. No one had ever jilted him before: *he* had always been the one to turn to fresh fields, younger blood. Or he had discovered some infidelity and made it a crafty excuse for a breach. Take Simone at the forge: he had been in and out of there, as one had to with machinery to mend, for years, then when her husband gave up the forge and set up the gas bottle and car accessories shop for Simone to run, so that he could devote himself to his land, she became much more easily accessible. It sufficed for her to hang a pillow-case – ostensibly to air – out of the second window from the right on the first floor of their house behind the shop, for Fernando to know that Raphaël her husband was gone for the day to tend the fields he had inherited from his parents.

Of course Simone was always 'on call' in the shop, but there were often long gaps in between customers. And what you couldn't get up to in the little store behind the spares showroom was nobody's business. There was even a quick way out through the back of the building, just in case.

Then one day, after something like six or seven years of this excellent arrangement, old Maurice ambled into the showroom while Fernando and Simone were steaming away with no holds barred in the back room. It was Maurice who ran the Judo club in the village and trained the young long-distance runners. Now everyone called him 'old' Maurice, although he was younger than Fernando. But he was short and stocky and, according to the girl who used to serve at one of the village shops, '*Fait comme un âne*'. This enviable anatomical feature had of course become the talk of the village, to Fernando's greatest chagrin, for he felt it like a slight on his own manliness, and from that moment on he viewed everything Maurice did with the utmost suspicion.

Simone reluctantly disentangled herself from their climactic embrace, smoothed down her skirt and did her best, dishevelled as she was, to look as if she had just run in from the garden behind the house, as she entered the glass-fronted showroom from the store room. Maurice had come in to look at batteries, he said, but the moment Simone came round the counter to show him what they had, he grabbed her round the waist and kissed her passionately, rubbing his body provocatively against hers. She made no serious move to push him away, but muttered something about people might see us. As indeed they did. For as Simone had rushed through the door to the store, Fernando had made sure it did not close completely by putting his foot in it. And what Fernando saw convinced him that Simone's relationship with Maurice involved more than selling him batteries. He went out the back way and walked briskly home to lunch, seething with anger and jealousy.

On his way back he called in at the petrol station to tell Simone that not only was he through with her but that if he ever – and he repeated *ever* – saw Maurice anywhere near her place, he would see to it that her husband knew all about it. 'Women!' he said to himself, as he rode off towards the farm, 'They think they can make a fool of me. Well, no one is going to do that to me: I'm cleverer than the lot of them. And as far as I'm concerned, there are plenty more fish in the sea; one more, one less, who cares?'

All that had been a long time ago, since Helen had come to live nearby shortly afterwards, and that had lasted nearly seven years. Then when he had tried to tear out the roses on the front of the house, all he got was a handful of thorns. In a rage, he hacked them down to ground level; by the following summer they were even more exuberant and fragrant than before the massacre and everyone begged him to leave them alone.

Eventually he managed to convince himself that he did not care. It wasn't as if he had not had many other irons in the fire, but apart from Dora, who lived in Sainte Pallarde, and who used to pick him up in her DS on Sunday afternoons when he was supposed to be out hunting, they were all local women or girls. Helen had been different: she was English, and not even old Maurice had that to boast about.

Fernando had been born in France, the seventh child of an Italian father, a carpenter by profession, who, with his wife and their first six children, had, like so many others round here, fled Mussolini's Italy to settle in France as a farmer in 1926. An eighth child, named Romeo, arrived a year after Fernando, who thus found himself lost in this gaggle of children, being neither the oldest nor the youngest.

His father made all their furniture, and they sat round the outsize dining-table always in order of precedence: father and mother together at the top, and the children in descending order of age, even numbers on the right, uneven on the left, which meant that Fernando, on opposite sides from his youngest brother, was always as far from his parents as he could be.

He was more or less brought up by his older siblings. He learnt to rely on no one but himself, and discovered that what you did not go out to get, no one was going to give you. His parents were strict and old-fashioned, but he quickly learnt to circumvent them whenever he wanted to, which was most of the time.

He lived close to nature and observed the habits and traces of every type of animal and bird. He knew every tree and bush capable of bearing edible fruit, knew the qualities and uses of every type of timber. He went to school and did well, for he and a girl, who went on to further education and later became a cardiologist, were the only pupils to obtain their school leaving certificate, which in those days you took at twelve, after which you were free to leave school if such was your parents' wish.

Such was his parents' wish, for they needed him on the farm. By then, most of the older boys had gone on to do other things. Two of his sisters had gone into service. The third had married. It had been a happy childhood, on the whole, though money was tight and you had to make do with what nature had to offer. Like girls.

Girls were taboo. And therefore all the more interesting. Girls in Italian families, such as he came from, were chaperoned, cloistered, protected, insulated, wrapped like precious china until a suitable husband was found and the knot tied. They slept in inviolable rooms, windows barred or windowless, rooms to which no one could accede except by passing through the parents' room.

So girls became his passion, and he spent his waking life dreaming up ways of outwitting the various mothers, aunts and other spoil-sports who kept him from laying a finger on their precious charges. At night he dreamed of the golden-haired girl with the budding breasts who smiled enigmatically whenever they met, or the fiery, insolent eyes of the little demon who lived with her grandmother on the edge of his village, with her curly black hair and smooth, white thighs, which she flashed at him willingly enough whenever the occasion arose. All he wanted was a bit of fun: there was no harm in that, was there, especially as his brothers had told him how to be 'careful' with a girl.

When he did his military service after the war was over – two years it was in those days – he discovered a very different world from the one he was used to. Girls, unaccompanied girls, were everywhere, and he soon forgot the embarrassment of having to admit to being a virgin. And, unlike most of his fellow conscripts, he was spared the ills that so often accompany promiscuity, and returned to his family convinced of his invulnerability and, of course, that he was God's gift to womankind.

Life in the army had taught him many things: how to live with others and pretend to like them when you didn't, how to wriggle out of awkward situations, how to wangle what you wanted, how to lie convincingly to save your skin. He had also grown stronger, more handsome and self-confident, although the little boy was still there, just under the skin and surprisingly vulnerable.

Back in the world of chaperoned girls, he decided that Nature required him to find himself a wife, preferably with a farm to work, since that was what he best understood. But while he was looking and enquiring, he used his best endeavours to seduce the black-haired girl with the sleek thighs. Not, he thought, that he would ever marry a girl like that: she was too hot by half, and would no doubt cuckold him whenever his back was turned. His wife must be above suspicion and preferably plain – not ugly, but definitely plain. She would be everlastingly grateful to him for saving her from spinsterhood, he felt sure.

He met Madeleine and proposed as soon as he had got to know her parents and been taken on a conducted tour of the property, such as it was. A pretty, old farmhouse with two bedrooms and a big kitchen leading out onto a pergola, shaded in summer by a grape vine. A beautiful, well-kept kitchen garden, the old man's pride and joy, an excellent well, twenty metres deep, and ten hectares of arable land, with more available if needed. The young couple would have the house and Madeleine's parents would move into the two-roomed cottage opposite, which was part of the property and did not need much to make it habitable again. There were no brothers or sisters, so it would all be theirs one day.

The wedding was planned, and meanwhile he found a way of climbing up to the first floor window where the black-haired girl slept, and would creep back home before dawn to do his work, taut as a crossbow all day till he saw the sun begin to sink towards the horizon and knew it would only be another hour or so until he stole back to those smooth white thighs. The night before his wedding he told the girl, as he pulled on his breeches, that it might be some time before he was able to come again.

Madeleine had been a good housekeeper and had borne him three daughters. But she had been frightened and tearful on their first night together, and endured his advances, as the years went by, with ever-increasing distaste, saying that he hurt her – she had always said that – and that surely, it was time they stopped all this kind of thing. He could never understand why others would clamour for more, seemed never to have had enough of him, while she clenched every muscle in her body, gritted her teeth and turned her head sideways on the pillow, her jaws locked, her eyes closed tight, until he leapt off her just before his climax, '*en faisant attention*', as his brothers had taught him was the way, or merely got bored at her total lack of response.

Madeleine used to enjoy talking to Helen when they first became acquainted. Helen lived just behind, but out of sight of, the old people's cottage, which she had to pass every time she went in or out. Once they found out that she spoke some French, they would often call her in for a chat. She loved them both, but in particular the old man, who had a very merry twinkle in his eye and a fund of fascinating stories to tell.

'My daughter doesn't understand men,' he said to her once, with a chuckle. 'Her mother didn't make a proper job of explaining what men are like, did you, Marietta?' He called across the table to his diminutive, shy wife, who merely smiled inscrutably back at him. 'Now you,' he went on, eyeing Helen with the gaze of a connoisseur, 'you know all about these things.' And Helen smiled back, thinking that it was a pity she had not met the old man in his prime.

Madeleine came in at that moment to fetch the basket for picking the supper vegetables, and Helen offered to help her: a moment's company might cheer her up a little, and in any case, she liked her, though did not feel as much at ease with her as with her parents.

'You know,' confided Madeleine as they finished picking a basket of ripe tomatoes, and wandered over to where the aubergines and peppers grew, 'I really don't care what Fernando gets up to – he's free to do what he likes, and does, believe me. But I just wish he would leave me alone. I wish he had someone who would really take the steam out of him, if you see what I mean. Are all men as demanding, I sometimes wonder?' And she gave a weary sigh as she half filled the second basket with fat peppers and shiny purple-skinned aubergines before turning to the courgettes that were beginning to spread beyond their allotted space.

Helen was quite taken aback by this burst of confidence, and was at a loss to know how to respond. But Madeleine gave her no time to reply.

'As you see,' she went on, searching for some of the larger courgettes, 'I'm going to make a ratatouille, and I thought I would freeze some for the winter. Do come and help yourself to all these vegetables whenever you like, won't you? I expect Fernando has already told you we have more than we can ever use. Feel free; they will only go to waste otherwise. He plants far too much.'

Helen felt sure that Madeleine had weighed her every word. She must know that Helen, living alone as she was, and so close to the farm, was an ideal target for her husband. Perhaps she thought their friendship might quieten him down.

There was scarcely a day when Fernando did not find a way of visiting Helen, and she got used to dropping whatever she was doing in order to spend with him whatever time he could spare. He hardly ever came empty-handed, but would arrive on foot, on his bicycle, or even occasionally on his beautiful blue motorbike, carrying a handful of new carrots, a few walnuts, a plastic bottle of his own wine, with a helpful tip about pruning, or planting vegetables, or looking after her hens, and always with the latest gossip. From their tracks, he would tell her what cars had been down her bit of driveway, and what animals had roamed about the place during the night. He was a fund of information about anything to do with the countryside, and knew everyone in the area, with all their foibles and weaknesses.

It gradually transpired that he had got to know, over the years, a large number of the local women and their daughters, having at some time or other persuaded, surprised or tricked them into playing his favourite game. He even told her of an occasional encounter, many years back, with a most respectable and well-known matron who, after being widowed, had called upon his 'services' from time to time, saying that it 'kept her normal', and offering him, after the event, a handsome, but completely unnecessary remuneration for his 'kindness'! Fernando seemed to be still as astonished as Helen was at this revelation, but it had a ring of authenticity, and she had no reason to doubt him.

This story lent credence to something Helen had once read, but found hard to believe at the time, not knowing France as well then as she now did, namely that there existed in Paris a number of discreet and admirably well-run brothels 'staffed' by men, and exclusively patronized, mainly in the afternoons, and with the utmost discretion, by the wives of men in high places, who tacitly sanctioned a 'sporting' activity that was, in their eyes, infinitely to be preferred to a 'liaison', an inevitable source of scandal.

Bit by bit Helen became aware that she was not the only pebble on Fernando's beach. True, she did not see why she should be, but it annoyed her to find him swearing black was white, while at the same time expecting her to sit at home like Penelope, awaiting his unscheduled arrivals. If she had to go out unexpectedly, and he called on her in her absence, he was visibly put out. He found it hard to accept that she had a life to lead of her own over which he in the nature of things had little or no control.

She brought a friend back once, clearly upset after a party that had ended very late, where candles, left alight in the room in which everyone had eaten, had set the table on fire, after burning down and melting their silver candlesticks while everybody was dancing in the next room. It had been a most unfortunate end to the evening, and she had agreed that another drink, preferably soft, and half an hour's quiet conversation in the calm of her home would help them both recover a sense of proportion after the disaster.

The man stayed half an hour. They talked. They drank a lot of Perrier. Then, saying he felt better, he left.

On his way back up Helen's short drive, he began to think its surface was even rougher than he had thought on driving down, and when he reached the tarmacked road he realized there was something seriously wrong with both his front tyres. After waiting for two hours for the nearest garage to open, he watched, incredulous, as six shiny, brand-new nails were removed from the tyres, which of course had been irremediably damaged by driving so far on the rough road.

Helen told Fernando exactly what had happened, but all he said was that people shouldn't go to that sort of party, which to her seemed a rather unsatisfactory response. For a nail left on the road for under an hour will show signs of incipient rust, and how did they miss them on the downward journey, anyway, arranged as they were to pierce both front tyres?

In fact, although Fernando continued to visit her daily, his possessiveness began to irk her, and when she told him she had a friend from England coming to stay for a few days, he said nothing, but she felt certain he was hanging around the house in the dark outside as they dined together in her big kitchen that evening.

The following morning as she passed the farm on her way to do some shopping, Fernando was waiting for her, his face like a mask, drawn and livid. She stopped her car and got out, naturally, to greet him, although she had never before seen him like this.

'Whatever's wrong?' she asked. 'You look awful. Are you ill, or something?'

'You know what's wrong,' came the answer. 'It's that man you've got there with you. I'll tell you this: either you get rid of him before this evening, or you won't see me again. You can take your choice.'

'Don't be so silly. You know perfectly well I can't send a visitor away just like that, and in any case it isn't your business. I'm not married to you and you have no right to tell me how to lead my life. So if that's the way it is, *tant pis*. Too bad. I'm sorry, but he's not going. Not just because you say so!' And she got back into her car, slammed the door, and drove on. She never spoke to him again.

Life in the village went on much as before, though Fernando's pride had been quite badly dented, and he had to make up for it by renewing old acquaintances and flaunting new conquests. But by now he was not as young as he had been, a fact that had not escaped some of the village girls who had only just started school at the time his own daughters were married.

'Good heavens, you're *old*, you are!' they would reply when he propositioned them blatantly.

'You should just try!' he would reply with a laugh. 'Then you'd find out whether I'm old or not. I'd show you a thing or two ... Better any day than those little whipper-snappers you go around with.'

And occasionally one or other of the young girls would run into him in a quiet lane, or some corner of the wood, and under the spell of his charm, her curiosity would get the better of her.

Of course there were occasions when his powers of persuasion – verbal, that is – were not quite adequate, and more pressing methods were required to achieve the desired result.

Occasionally he found himself confronted by angry husbands or fathers whose daughters had said horrible things about him. But having learnt at an early age that to lie convincingly requires you to believe in the truth of what you are saying, he somehow managed to convince them, and himself, of his utter innocence, and they went away apologizing for their unfortunate mistaken accusations.

But as he accumulated occasions when he was obliged to resort to these strategies, little by little word got around that he was not to be trusted. They had laughed at his excesses for a long time, for he was one of them: a good sort, basically. And no one had got hurt, at any rate not so that you would know. But now, they were beginning to feel that it was time he stopped.

Then one day the village chemist let drop the fact that someone in the local doctor's practice had been diagnosed as HIV positive. No, of course, professional secrecy forbad the doctor naming names, and the practice was a large one, but the doctor had told him he knew of someone. You could not be too careful nowadays, with things as they were, could you?

It was not long after this news had got around that Fernando's shiny blue motorbike was burnt to a cinder during the night.

When he rode off that morning on his bicycle to the farm to let the hens out, scarcely a soul greeted him. The old cobbler on the corner, the shopkeeper opening his shutters, even Henriette from the café, sweeping the pavement before putting the chairs and tables outside, all seemed subdued, distant, as if trying to avoid him.

What on earth was the matter with them all, he wondered. After all, he'd done nothing wrong, had he? It wasn't his fault if some bastard had destroyed his precious motorbike. Just because he enjoyed a bit of fun!

But the village, like all small communities, I suspect, having been almost unanimous in their acceptance of Fernando with all his charm, and in spite of his rumoured excesses, now suddenly considered that enough was enough. It was almost certainly some quite other person the doctor had been referring to when he had mentioned the matter to the chemist, but the effect was the same. Fernando had been blackballed, and life would never be quite the same again for him in La Motte.

XV   Village Gossip, and Two Soirées

Village communities are cruel in this way: people say all kinds of things about you, but never to your face. I am sure that lots of things were said about me that never reached my ears, for better or for worse! And conversely, I myself became party to much village gossip. I knew who wouldn't speak to whom and why, who poached game outside the hunting season, who was up to his neck in debt, even who scrubbed out his pesticide-drenched sprayer tank in the local stream.

I knew, for instance, along with almost everyone else in the village, that while the charming old tippler who ran the 'Cafe de la Halle' was left on his own to cope with his customers every Tuesday afternoon, Henriette, his hard-working, pretty wife went shopping in town, some twenty minutes' drive away. And that it wasn't only shopping she did. For when I eventually managed to buy an old car, and became more mobile, I used to bump into her there from time to time, usually as she emerged from the best patisserie, two luscious creamy concoctions in a small open-topped box dangling from her forefinger by its loop of spiralling pink ribbon. She would greet me, explaining bright-eyed and with a merry laugh that pâtisseries were her *péché mignon*, a weakness she could not resist, and that it was just as well she only came to town on Tuesdays. What she did not mention, of course, was her other *péché mignon*, who was waiting in their discreet back-street hotel bedroom for *his* pâtisserie to arrive ...

When someone in the Commune dies, the church bell is tolled immediately for five minutes or so, again in the evening and again before the funeral, which takes place the day after the death, or at

128

the outside, on the second day. Now a certain woman in La Motte was on her deathbed some years ago. Shortly before she died she expressed a last wish: that the bell should not be tolled for her by the person who usually did it.

Consternation all round, but a person's last wishes had to be carried out to the letter. Our bell was normally tolled by an elderly woman who lived next to the church, and held the key to the big west door; when she was asked for the key and told that someone else would take over the bell-ringing on this particular occasion, she refused to hand it over, saying that no one else was going to touch 'her' bell!

Of course everyone knew that the dead woman and the bell-ringer had not spoken for years, not since the war, in fact. For while the bell-ringer's husband had been deported to Germany, the dead woman's husband, who was fortunate enough to have remained at home, made good his neighbour's absence by spending whatever time he could with the lonely grass widow, to the no small annoyance of his own wife.

It took several hours of gentle persuasion by the village priest to get the church key from the bell-ringer and convince her that it would be best if he himself tolled the bell on his occasion, and that was what they eventually agreed. But the regular bell-ringer refused ever to do it again and in the end the municipal council had to have the bell mechanized. Such are village quarrels.

I tried my utmost not to get involved, even peripherally, in these kind of disputes, but tended to find that, unless people were told everything about you, and indeed even if they were, they would fabricate all manner of fanciful tales, which would rapidly become common currency in the village.

Claude Boniface, for instance, not, one has to admit, one of the brighter intellects in our village, was forever asking me where my husband was. As I had no intention of discussing my marital problems with him, I would say that he was 'travelling', which was indeed sometimes the case, since he regularly visited a number of countries in connection with his work and research projects.

'What country?' he would ask. And I would reply 'Switzerland', or 'Spain', or on one occasion, 'Romania'. How misguided I was to tell him the literal truth, for within a week I heard that Claude Boniface was telling everybody that I was 'married to a spy'!

My large number of books caused much misunderstanding, too, for few, if any, of the people I knew read anything other – if indeed they read at all – than what everyone around here calls *Le Journal*, in other words our local daily paper, *Le Sud-Ouest*. And if one took *Le Journal*, whatever could one possibly need all those books for?

I heard a story not long ago about the wholesale burning of documents, records and registers during the Revolution of 1789, when the ordinary people of towns and villages attacked the seats of power and burned every parchment, map and picture they could lay their hands on. It appears that in our local town the bonfire burned for eight days while every existing record went up in smoke.

Not quite all, however, for some peasant farmers, alerted by the smoke and flames, came into the little town and 'rescued' some of the piles of parchment from the pyre. For in those days as now, the local priest would be invited to eat with various families from time to time, and the priest from one of the surrounding parishes, who had managed to survive the revolutionary purges, while on a visit to one of the families, spotted some sheets of parchment that were being used as lids to cover the *toupines de confit*, the large stone jars in which chicken, goose and duck pieces were (and still are) preserved under a deep coating of fat. Thereafter he always carried circles of parchment with him, exchanging them for the priceless pages from the archives that had survived in this so ironical a manner. In my more cynical moments I sometimes wonder how much things have really changed since then!

The isolation I experienced was not at all as it must have been in the past generations. For even though it took seven years to obtain a telephone when I arrived (thanks to Giscard d'Estaing's efforts it now takes a couple of days at most and France's telephone system is at the moment one of the most advanced in the world, after being one of the most primitive), I nevertheless did have electricity and piped water in addition to my well. So I could listen to records, then tapes, and the radio played loud and clear at the turn of a button. I even treated myself to a second-hand black and white television set with a tiny electronic aerial in the loft to save spoiling the sleek lines of the roof. And since I was on the top of a hill, this arrangement worked perfectly well, and I learnt an enormous amount of the kind of French my university studies had never taught me.

As for water, the well water supplied the kitchen, since it was very pure and always at the same temperature. A small pump, immersed in the well, brought it up as required into a tall pressurized storage tank in the barn, and thence to the kitchen sink. But the mains water fed the bathroom and loo, since I thought the quantities needed might have unduly strained the capacities of a well that was reputed, according to Gaston, to have once actually dried up, in 1947, when the whole of France suffered an almost catastrophic drought. This was confirmed by the Jeanblanc 'boys', whose cows, unable to obtain the forty litres of water they each required per day, had to be sold for slaughter at knock-down prices. The wine was of top quality that year, of course, but I fear where wine was concerned its quality was not what mattered most to the Jeanblanc family.

I was, culturally speaking, hibernating in my lonely house, I suppose one might say. Licking my wounds, feeling my way gently into my new life. But I was happy. Happy to be alive. Happy to be surrounded by such beauty, such harmony, and to find myself so much in sympathy with my surroundings. There were, apart from my domestic animals, a host of other creatures that became

familiar friends: the little green frogs that sang at the approach of rain, a number of lovely old toads that roamed the garden at night, vivid salamanders basking in the sun by day, and, of course, hundreds of lizards that would cock their heads on one side as you talked or whistled to them.

Once an enormous caterpillar fell out of the walnut tree onto my skirt: it must have been a good six inches long and the hairs that covered its almost luminous lime-green body looked like so many black hatpins, each one ending in a bright blue knob. It was the most alarmingly colourful creature I had ever just missed having in my hair, and I eventually saw its transformation through the chrysalis stage into a huge moth with gorgeous blue wings that spanned fifteen centimetres. I did find out what it was: apparently the biggest European moth, though its name has now escaped me, since it was very long and in Latin. Unfortunately it did not seem to have a common name, or I might have remembered it!

The occasional deer would be seen in the fields or the neighbouring vines, and one evening as the full moon was rising over the distant hills, some wild boar snorted their way through my orchard and made off into Fernando's maize. Snakes, too, were not uncommon around the house, though discouraged by my keeping the immediate surroundings clear of odd stones or other debris, and, of course, keeping the grass short. I did not mind the large, swift-moving grass snakes: these sometimes reached a considerable length and would live in holes in the ground, often in a clump of bamboos or a small coppice. They were quite harmless, but would surprise me by their sheer speed. Vipers, on the other hand, were smaller, slower and potentially dangerous, especially if you happened to tread on one, or disturb it as it warmed itself among a pile of stones. The local people never left their house doors or windows open for fear that a snake might take refuge in the house. The *Mémé* Boniface told me once how, during the war, she had been bitten by a viper she had accidentally introduced into the house on a log intended for the fire. She had been over a week in hospital on that occasion.

But little by little I became fascinated by the people who surrounded me, be they peasant farmers of Gascon, Breton or Italian origin, immigrants from other parts of France or indeed from the UK, Holland or America, and eventually, the small town bourgeoisie, although here, with one or two notable exceptions, I felt less at ease.

The retired doctor from our nearest small town – the one who had delivered the Jeanblanc children when the family inhabited my house – asked me to what he called *une réception* in his handsome, bourgeois home. His wife had been the chemist in the town – an excellent, rewarding partnership, one might well say – and I have to admit that I didn't quite know what to expect. Their house was exquisitely furnished: priceless antiques side by side with the very best of modern furniture, the kind of thing that only Paris can provide in its most up-market shops. A delight for the eye.

After consuming generous drinks of the cocktail party variety, accompanied by delectable tiny sausage rolls, asparagus sandwiches and smoked salmon vol-au-vents, just as I was beginning to think it was time to go, we were ushered into a further room, where new glasses were filled with the finest champagne and we were invited to approach a table laden with a magnificent buffet supper.

The guests were mostly French, with a scattering of English, very few of whom I had ever met, so although I did my utmost to be sociable, I nevertheless felt that a reasonable degree of reserve was *de rigueur* in company like this, for I sensed a certain distance that came between me and anyone to whom I admitted to living alone. On one occasion the doctor's wife joined in and told the assembled company how terribly brave she thought I was, living in such an isolated, lonely house, as if the ten kilometres that separated her house from mine put me in another world. I suppose it did, actually. And although I appreciated being asked, I was glad to get back to my own world again.

Another encounter I had with the 'other side' of provincial France, was being invited to a soirée at a local vet's home. I had met him when I had taken my cats to be doctored. The male, Zig, posed no problems, but the female's operation was of course, more extensive and delicate. Puce had managed to produce four kittens, two of which I kept for want of another home for them, and two I managed to give away to more or less willing recipients. It is very hard to find homes for kittens in the country, since no one here ever sterilizes their cats – it costs too much, they say – and kittens are regularly drowned whenever they appear, even at several weeks old when the wary mother has given birth to them in some well hidden cache.

My wily little Puce managed to escape from the house when I

thought she still had several days to go before coming on heat for the second time. This was when I had intended to take her to the vet. But she was gone for three days, before slinking home covered in mud and ravenously hungry. I calculated that the new kittens would be born in August.

Then early in July I developed viral hepatitis and was extremely ill, all alone there with my four cats and, by then, a large number of rabbits. And by the time I was just beginning to stagger round the house to attend to the most basic needs of my animals and myself, Puce had four more kittens, each one black and white just like her. There was nothing for it but to drown them immediately. It was the most terrible thing I have ever been required to do, and I still think with horror of the awfulness of it, while tears run down my face as I write.

Poor little Puce wandered miserably mewing round the house for the next two days, then vanished up a long ladder onto a kind of shelf that ran round part of the barn. She refused to come down for food, but obstinately hid herself behind a cardboard box that had somehow been stored out of reach up there.

Late that evening I went out to the barn again in the hope of persuading her to come down to eat, when I thought I heard a thin mewing from the shelf. In the end I ventured up the ladder, still more than wobbly-legged, and to my utter astonishment found a purring Puce nursing a solitary new-born all-black kitten inside the cardboard box.

What could I do but tell her what a clever cat she had been, to have produced this kitten forty-eight hours after the others, and how delighted I was to see her happy again, and that her food was waiting whenever she felt like it. I also told her during the following days that we would go to the vet together as soon as she had finished nursing her new kitten, who was to be called Epigone – Last born – or Piggy for short. So then I had five cats.

After living as I have for so long, I have become acutely aware of life in all its many manifestations, and more and more loath to take it, even when the creature concerned is potentially harmful. Spiders are discouraged from living in the house by spraying the scent of chestnut wood, which they don't care for. (Many old houses round here have chestnut flooring to their lofts, and you never see spiders on the ceilings or in the rooms below.) Wasps usually go elsewhere if you don't flap at them in a panic. There is nothing so soft as the wings of a wasp brushing your arm or your hand before it takes off to investigate something more rewarding than a piece of human skin. You just mustn't crush them, that's all, because they don't like it, and can you blame them?

When.eventually Puce and I visited the vet for her operation, she was surprisingly good, considering her wild origins and very rural environment. Neither she nor the other cats needed to come into the living quarters of the house, for they had my enormous barn to live in, where they were free to come and go, day and night, and where their mere presence kept the mice away. So catching her and putting her in a borrowed cat basket was far from easy, but she settled down during the journey and allowed herself to be anaesthetized by this total stranger without protest. I was told to return for her towards the evening.

The vet must have thought I was reasonably civilized, since he asked me whether I would like to join him and his wife and a few local friends for an evening get-together about a fortnight from then. He referred to the gathering as *le cercle*, which I must admit was a word I had heard but the precise meaning of which eluded me.

He was a funny man: blunt and plain-spoken, and a bit inclined to put a hand on you for no obvious reason. He made a point of talking in somewhat coarse terms of the finer points of artificial insemination, getting stallions 'ready' for mating, and other topics that could be bracketed under the same heading. I met his wife a week later when I took Puce over again to have her stitches out, and she talked to me in the waiting room while her husband dealt with Puce.

She was a strange woman, totally unlike her husband: one of those women who bewail their fate in life from the moment they set eyes on you, with every imaginable detail of their miseries exposed to your view, like it or not, so that you are reduced to a kind of machine pouring out exclamations of sympathy and compassion with clockwork regularity until her flood of woes is interrupted by some external agent.

Fortunately Puce was not long with her husband, though she had time to tell me the horrors of her wedding night – which must have been at least twenty-five years ago – when her husband, obsessed by the attack of pneumonia his *guenon* (such a wonderful word for a female monkey) was suffering from, had insisted that the creature share their bed so that together they could keep her warm!

I must confess I found it hard to keep a straight face when she came out with this, and it is true to say that although in my time I have heard some pretty strange complaints from wives about their husbands, and indeed from husbands about their wives, this particular moan gets first prize for originality! '*Imaginez-vous, Madame, une Guenon dans mon lit de noces!*' And said with such emotion, her lip trembling at the memory. She had not many hopes left that her rough-and-ready husband had not dashed, and she clung so desperately to her notion of how things should be ordered in life, yet in hers were not.

So I had some reservations about the soirée, and went along not knowing which of the spouses I would prefer not to have to talk to! I hoped that there would be other guests present to add leaven to the mix.

There were indeed fourteen of us gathered round in a circle, seated on straight-backed, elegant but rather hard chairs and narrow two-seater settees, upholstered in satin but making few concessions to comfort, as befitted the ancient bourgeois tradition. But at least the lights were dim, which gave an illusion of comfort.

As everyone seemed to know everyone else our host introduced me to the company at large, telling them everything he knew about me, which I felt could be of no possible interest to most of them, particularly as most of it was sheer speculation on his part. I felt annoyed and embarrassed. We were served strong drinks, followed by *petits fours* and coffee, then people began to move around and talk more freely. To judge from their expensive clothes, they all seemed to be from the middle classes: there were two good-looking couples in their forties, three elegant women between thirty and thirty-five, apparently unattached, three men of indeterminate age on their own, and one very young man. Our hosts and I made up the fourteen.

I must confess that I could not think what brought this particular group of people together. My host the vet, a blunter man still than I had at first thought possible, joined me on one of the tiny settees and suddenly began asking me a string of the most personal and impertinent questions: what was my sex life like? Did I take the pill? Did I still have good legs? (I was wearing smart trousers for the occasion) I felt like a cow being gone over by the judges at a show ground. Then suddenly everything fell into place: these people were looking at me as a potential candidate to join their *cercle*, the activities of which were purely and simply orgiastic. A daisy chain, *une partouze*.

I pleaded a bad headache – felt like flu coming on, I said, and made my escape with a sigh of relief. And when the time came for Puce's kitten Piggy to have her op., I went to another vet.

XVI   The Foxes' Lair

Some time after I settled at La Motte an unusual family came to live in an old, dilapidated house between the Boniface family farm and the village. I met them by accident, and found them quite different from any family I had ever come across before: a law unto themselves, one might say, even though I am beginning to feel that this formula applies to a surprisingly large number of Frenchmen!

One morning our cheerful, lackadaisical postmaster was sitting behind his polished wooden counter, listening to *France Inter* to while away the time between customers. His wife had left the breakfast dishes to give him a hand with the sorting, while her charge, a year-old baby girl, whose mother worked full-time as the chemist's assistant, foraged in the waste paper basket for whatever treasures she could reach. There was a man in the post office, too, a man I had never seen before, gesticulating as he struggled to make himself understood over the public telephone.

In those days, the only public telephone in the village was inside the post office, which greatly restricted its usefulness. This was still further limited by the fact that it had no door, which meant that every word spoken into the handset became common knowledge throughout the village, with greater or lesser accuracy, within four hours at the outside from the time it was uttered.

But the problem seemed to be of a different order, and after a few more tries, the stranger gave up, with elaborate expressions of regret, and put the phone down.

'How much do I owe you?' he asked the postmaster in an accent that was unmistakably Paris. The sort of Parisian that turns all its *a*s into *o*s and delivers them from the very depths of the throat, while nasalizing most of the other sounds into a thin, clipped prattle, patently unintelligble to the postmaster or to his wife, who peered curiously at the stranger from between the fronds of her philodendron that clambered over the decorative wire mesh separating the tiny area reserved for customers from the somewhat larger part of the room in which the 'real' work like weighing and franking letters went on.

'*Combien?*' the man repeated, holding out a hundred franc note.

'Do you realize,' the Postmaster said, turning to me, 'that I understand him less well than I understand you? And considering you're English ... I don't seem to get anywhere with these foreigners from the North.'

And that was how I met the head of the Fennec family.

'*Anglaise! Vous êtes anglaise?*' the stranger cried, jumping up and down with excitement. 'What a piece of luck!' he exclaimed, seizing my arm. 'You see, Madame,' he confided, 'I've just been trying to talk to an English friend but somehow I can't make him understand. It's OK when we are face to face, but on the telephone ... *absolument impossible!*'

The postmaster seemed astonished that I was able to understand the man when he couldn't, and gave a shrug of resignation as he handed the stranger his change.

'*Non, non! Gardez-le.* Keep it for the moment. I'm going to try again if this good lady will agree to help me. *Venez, Madame. Je vais vous expliquer.*'

So, grasping my arm in his, he led me out of the post office and walked me at the double round the square, explaining that he wanted to talk to this old friend, and hear whatever news he had, but did not want him to know where he was, at least not precisely. He would explain all that later, but please would I be so good as to translate what he said into English and say it to his friend? And not to mention the name of the village, or the *département* for that matter.

Back we went into the post office, where the postmaster still sat clutching the change from the first call. The number was duly rung again, and Monsieur Fennec, as he told me he was called – Louis Fennec, but please call me Louis – Monsieur Fennec said: '*Re-bonjour, John. Attendez un instant ...*' and handed me the receiver.

After a few necessary explanations about who I was and what I was doing there I duly translated everything Louis Fennec said to me, which in the end seemed to amount to little more than chit-chat: he and his family had found and bought a house – pretty tumble-down, but they would work on it – and everything was going well. No, they had no telephone (no one did in those days) and he was not too sure of their address. But he promised to keep in touch from time to time. Yes, Monique was well, and all the children, though it was quite a job to keep all that lot fed and clothed. They would have to put their names down for school next September. It was too late to bother this year, and in any case he was going to need their help in restoring the house. Yes, they would probably start with the roof. Always the most important, the roof. But in a couple of months, say by the end of June, they should manage that, then they would set about making the inside more comfortable. And how was the *garrigue*? Still as wild and unpopulated as ever? He missed that sort of countryside where he now was, but it wasn't possible to stay on there, was it, with all the local people ganging up on him the way they had begun to do. Goodness knows what for. He never did anybody any harm, did he? Never mind, though. France is a big place and there's room for all sorts, isn't there? Yes, he would keep in touch. He was not one to forget his old friends.

It wasn't easy to keep up with him, since Louis Fennec spoke, as he moved, at the double, and did not allow me enough time to listen to his friend's reply, let alone translate it. But the result seemed to satisfy him; at any rate he showered thanks on me and, when he found that I lived only about a kilometre up the hill from his house, being, like him, a neighbour of the Boniface family, he gave many an earnest invitation to come and see them. There was always someone there, he assured me, and his wife would be delighted, too, to meet someone as *sympathique* as me.

I must confess I had certain reservations about Louis Fennec, but felt that the reasons for his move were no concern of mine. Before I got round to taking up his impetuous invitation, he and his wife Monique turned up on foot one afternoon as I was planting a few potatoes in the vegetable patch. Scarcely stopping to introduce his wife, he asked me whether I had any feathers. An extraordinary question, it seemed to me, coming totally out of the blue like that, but even more strangely, perhaps, I happened to have a bagful in the barn, collected and not yet burned after plucking two chickens the previous evening. So at his request I fetched them and he put a large fistful in my trench where each potato was to go, planted the potatoes and covered them over with earth.

'There!' he exclaimed. 'That's done! Didn't you know about feathers for planting potatoes? Lets them breathe. You'll see: you'll get far more tubers when you give them room to grow. Just you wait and see. You'll never do it any other way after trying this.'

Monique was a smiling, cheerful woman, just turned forty, she told me, while her husband was nearly fifty. In France your date of birth is pretty well common knowledge, figuring as it does on all your papers, from your identity card which, though not obligatory, is a most useful document to have about you, to your social security card that proves your entitlement to reimbursement of medical expenses. She obviously relished telling me about how she had once been a champion basket-ball player (perhaps the 'once' accounted for the considerable gain in weight, which she disguised under a flowing caftan-type garment) and how Louis had said, when he proposed marriage to her, that it was to be him or basket-ball. He wanted a wife who remained at home and looked after all the children he intended to have. So she had made her choice and there they were. No regrets. And six children: a girl, now sixteen, then five boys of eleven, ten, nine, eight and seven.

Louis told me he had been in the Foreign Legion. I had never before met a légionnaire and had only the sketchiest of notions about who they were and how they came to join. All I had heard was that they led a tough life, under an implacable discipline, in return for which no questions were asked about their origins, nationality or life history.

The Fennec habit of doing everything at the double had clearly been transmitted to the children, who scurried hither and thither under their father's orders. Their manners were beyond reproach, even when their father was well out of sight: somewhat unusual these days, I thought. I never did manage to sort out which was Serge, which Geoffrey, or Victor, or Boris, or Marius, but was endlessly amused at the way they would raise their five little cotton caps as one man and chant in unison: '*Bonjour, Madame!*' whenever we met. It was slightly disconcerting to run into them all quite so frequently in or near my garden, but they always seemed to be well-behaved and very friendly, asking how I was and if they could help me in any way, so I saw no reason to complain.

When Louis decided it was time to begin work on the roof, he lined the boys up and told them what he expected of them: they were to position themselves along the ridge and follow his instructions to the letter. In due course the first part of the roof was stripped of its heavy *tuiles canal* – which were stacked further along, waiting to be replaced as each section was strengthened, all to orders rapped out by Louis, whose feet remained securely anchored to the ground. It was quite a sight to see the five small boys, dwarfed even further for being looked at from so far below, gradually produce a clean, flat, evenly-tiled surface from what had been an irregularly sagging, moss-covered, and badly leaking roof.

While the boys were busy on the roof, Louis told me, with actions to illustrate his words, how the long *tuiles canal* used to be made before the days of automation. 'You see,' he said, cupping his hands into an arch, 'the *chapeau* is of course the tile that goes over the *courant*, the one that forms the gully' – here he inverted the arch – 'and lets the water drain away. Well, the *chapeau* has of course to be wider than the *courant*, in order to cover it properly. They're both the same length, of course, about 50 cm, though of course when they are properly laid, you only see a third of each tile, the rest is covered by the next tile and so on – if you see what I mean.' Here his hands began to play leap-frog over one another. 'This stops rainwater backing-up under the *chapeau*.'

I knew his story about the tiles, but did not have the heart to cut him off in full flight: he so loved talking, and above all, giving instructions and explanations. His children probably learnt more from working at home than they ever would at school, though I was beginning to have certain reservations about some of the things they seemed to be learning. But, I told myself, it takes all sorts to make a world, and perhaps my life style was as puzzling to them as theirs was to me. But there still was a great deal I could not understand about the Fennec family.

'So you see,' Louis went on, 'they needed two different moulds for the two types of tiles, and what did they use? Legs, of course. Thighs! Can't you see it? Scrawny men's thighs to mould the clay for the *courant* and a good solid woman's thigh for the *chapeau!*' I couldn't help laughing, as he slapped his own thigh, then Monique's through her caftan, as if wrapping them about with a thick layer of clay; and although I had been told this story before, I enjoyed seeing the sheer delight it gave him to tell it.

The Fennec daughter, Angèle, was not as cheerful as her father. She seemed to spend her time sweeping the house: a thankless task with all the work on the roof going on. In any case, the interior needed to be completely rebuilt: as it stood it was all right to camp in during the summer months, but needed a great deal of work before the following winter set in.

'No! it's not like that! That's not the way to sweep with one of those brooms!' Louis exclaimed, as his daughter, brushing away vigorously at the old tiled floor, seemed to be raising more dust than she was collecting.

'Look!' he went on, grasping the big flat-headed broom. 'Look, it's like this. Goodness knows how often I've told you before. You must *stroke* it along the floor and not allow a single strand of the broom to flip up in the air at the end of each stroke. Do you see? Now try it again. For Heaven's sake, girl, if I'd raised dust like that when I was in the Légion, I'd have been court-martialled!'

Perhaps his daughter was wishing he had, but she just went on sweeping, with neither a word nor a smile. I wondered what kind of life it was for her now she had left school, for she seemed to be needed at home and clearly had no other projects in view.

It was not a farm the Fennecs had bought, scarcely even a smallholding, having only about an acre of uncultivated land and another acre with poplars on it. The poplars were about half grown, so they had a good ten more years to go before they would bring in any money. As for the land, it was low-lying like the house, and would probably produce enough vegetables for their needs, and a patch of maize for hens, without costing them a fortune in watering during the summer. Next to them on one side were fields belonging to the Boniface family, whose two houses stood about a kilometre further out of the village, and on the other side were several small plots of land belonging to various inhabitants of the village itself. The plot that adjoined the Fennecs' fence swarmed with guinea-fowl, their wings clipped to prevent them flying away, and their scowling owner, manifestly disapproving of his new neighbours, came down the road from the village daily to feed and tend his precious table birds.

I must confess it did occur to me to wonder sometimes how the Fennecs lived, although with six children you could just about get by on family allowances, provided you owned your house and grew your food. Vegetables they had in plenty, but as yet they seemed to have no hens or rabbits like other people in the village.

One day, however, I got quite a surprise. I was walking down the hill from my house through the fields, and had reached the point where, for a brief moment, I had a panoramic view of the

Fennecs' house. Everything seemed peaceful. They must all be inside. Perhaps now the roof was finished, the boys were beginning on the interior, with their father, as always, providing the instructions, while they laboured like navvies. It was not everyone's idea of how to bring up children, but they did seem to be growing up cheerful and happy – with perhaps the exception of Angèle – and infinitely resourceful. And their manners never failed to astonish me.

Then suddenly a shot rang out, crisp and clear and unmistakable in the quiet of the summer noon. As if out of nowhere, a little Fennec leapt out of the house, having been catapulted, it seemed, across the garden, so quickly did he move; he vaulted the fence, and in one second flat, leapt back again into his own garden, clutching a stricken guinea-fowl. And all fell still once more, the silence all the heavier for having been so rudely shattered by Louis's single rifle shot. I turned back home unseen, not wanting them to know I had witnessed this dubious episode.

When the interior improvements were well under way, I was invited to see what they were doing to the house, and to stay for a simple family lunch if I would care to. Why not, I thought, hoping that guinea-fowl would not figure on the menu. I need have had no such fears, for our lunch was a bowl of savoury rice with a salad and fruit, just the sort of thing I loved, but all too rarely seen on French tables, particularly in our part of France. But then the Fennecs were not from our part of France, and in any case had their own very clear ideas about how they wanted to lead their lives.

As for the way they were tackling the house, I was filled with admiration, for, instead of the perfectly horrible 'modernization' so often perpetrated by the local French at that time, here was a real attempt to keep the old features and materials of the original house and to respect its history. Generations of green paint had been carefully peeled away from their two ancient fireplaces, revealing stones as golden and perfect as the day they were cut. A little oval *œil de boeuf* had been lovingly uncovered and cleaned, and a tiny pane of glass carefully puttied inside to keep out draughts while letting in the sunshine.

The old stone sink, set in the wall of the principal room, had been cleared of all the rubble and planks with which some former owner had tried to block it up, and sat proudly in its niche with a huge bowl resting in it, full of teasels and bulrushes, their spiky silhouettes softened by a cloud of cow-parsley. The tiled floors had been taken up with infinite care, tile by tile – a colossal task – and re-laid, not on bare earth as before, but on a screed poured over a waterproof sheeting. With their new joints there would be little dust, once they had settled down; this would surely please Angèle, would it not? But Angèle just nodded and went back to her thoughts.

After our simple, excellent lunch, Monique and Louis showed me the converted loft upstairs, pointing out all the work they had done and what remained to be done. They feared that when the children had to begin school it would slow down the renovations, but she had already had the authorities after her, saying that the boys should have been registered earlier. The Fennecs clearly hated any form of interference with their chosen life style.

It was some time later that summer that I fell ill. I had had a friend from England to stay, and drove her to Merignac airport in my newly acquired little car for her return flight. It was an exceptionally hot day with the thermometer on the motorway registering forty, and I felt extremely tired when I got home. By the evening I was feeling weak-kneed and light-headed, so decided bed was best. By the morning, bed was not only best, it was the only place for me, as I was unable to get up. I was not even hungry. I was very ill.

Later that day I managed to open my bedroom shutters and hoped that eventually someone would come looking for me, so that I could ask them to fetch a doctor. It is hard to imagine it now, but in those days it was not uncommon for people to have to wait for over ten years to get a telephone installed. Needless to say, I was still waiting.

Then suddenly the window grew dark with a cluster of little faces, as the Fennec boys, surprised at not finding me in the garden, crowded round the only window whose shutters were open, to see if I happened to be there.

'*Oh! Dites-donc! Elle est toute jaune! Comme un citron!*' I heard them exclaim to one another. I had not realized that my face had gone lemon-yellow, but the doctor, when he came that evening, took matters in hand. Not that there is anything much one can do about hepatitis, except to try to avoid getting it oneself.

The Fennecs offered to do my shopping. But I had everything I

needed, since I could not face food at all at first. Louis alarmed me
by offering to give me the course of injections the doctor had
prescribed (heavens knows why!) They had taught them, *dans la
Légion*, to give injections – yes, even intravenous ones – so why
pay the nurse to do something as simple as that? I was rather glad
to be able to say thank you but no, the nurse had already begun
the course, so I could hardly interrupt it, could I? I wondered what
else the *Légion* might have taught Louis to do, and the notion
brought me little comfort, ill as I was.

A couple of months later the Fennec boys started school. I was
quite glad not to have them hanging around my place day after
day, even though they often helped with this and that, particularly
things that I still felt too exhausted to do. I had lost nearly two
stone and my trousers and skirts hung about my hips like
rain-sodden washing on a line. But the mere thought of eating
anything less bland than plain boiled potatoes seemed still to make
me feel quite ill. Granny Boniface, my nearest neighbour down
the hill, had clambered up through the fields with a hen she had
killed and prepared for me. Such a very kind thought. But when
she grinned at me and said: '*Je vous ai apporté une belle poule bien
grasse*,' stressing the word *grasse* (she had brought me a lovely fat
hen), the word 'fat' itself made my stomach turn over. Strange
how the liver can play up.

   I have always thought that if you are going to eat meat, you
should be realistic about how it is slaughtered and prepared. Most
of us will visit the butcher's happily enough, or, if we dislike the
sight of hanging carcasses, will buy ready-packed meat from a
supermarket. But visiting a slaughter-house is another matter.
And when you breed rabbits and keep hens, if it is your intention
to eat them, then they have to be killed, gutted, skinned or
plucked, and there is no escaping the harsh brutality of it all.

   I had not by then begun to sell my 'produce' to the local
charcutier and my rabbit cages were bursting with life by the time I
felt well enough to deal with them. Loyal friends from the next
village had cut grass for the inmates daily and given them water.
But the tiny new babies that had been born two days before I fell
ill, were by now themselves almost adult, and desperately required
more space. I was going to have to cull some of the older ones, a
job I always hated doing, such charming creatures they were. And
my illness did nothing to fortify my resolve. So when I saw the

Fennec boys, I asked them whether their mother would care for some rabbits, in exchange for killing and preparing some for me.

When Monique came up to the house I let her get on with the job, which she did swiftly and expertly, while I merely wrapped the prepared rabbits for the freezer and thanked her warmly for her help. She went away with a breeding pair to start their own supply, and a couple of older ones she had killed while in the barn. She asked if she might take all the skins, and, as I could not see myself trying to tan them at that moment, I was only too pleased to let her have them.

It was after this that I noticed I had mislaid some odd tools, and began to search high and low, wondering when I had last used them, and surprised that they were not in their usual place, since the workshop was usually tidy. And, of course, I hadn't had occasion to use anything for several weeks.

Then the boys came up one morning, entering the house through the barn, instead of coming round to the kitchen door as they usually did. We had a short chat and some orange squash together, and they went on their way. It was that evening that I needed my steel rule, knowing full well where I had left it that very morning. It was not there. And neither was one of my screwdrivers. This time there could be no doubt that there were people helping themselves to my tools. Nothing big, like my electric drill, but I was now certain that things were disappearing, and the discovery made me feel deeply uncomfortable. I could hardly accuse the Fennec boys, or their mother, for that matter. I had no proof, only it could not have been anyone else, since no one other than the five little boys had been near the place that day.

I felt betrayed. I was going to have to keep everything under lock and key, or not admit any of them to the house. But then, what about the hens, the bantams and the ducks? I began to think I was hearing noises at night, and found I was only dozing instead of sleeping deeply as I usually did. How sad, to have misjudged people, failed to understand them, when the indications had been there, after all. I felt a fool, but what could I do, except make sure I gave them no further opportunities to steal from me.

For a month or so after that we did not meet. Then suddenly one morning, almost before I was up, all five boys were there, as cheerful as ever, knocking at the kitchen door.

'*Bonjour, Madame!* We're ever so sorry to come round so early,' they began, 'but Mother wondered if you could go down as soon as you're up and about. We're off to school now. The term began last week.'

'Oh, so you're going to school now, are you?' I replied. 'Have you made some friends?'

'Not many,' replied the biggest of the boys. 'We prefer being at home. Don't forget, will you; Mother says it's urgent.'

'I won't forget,' I reassured them with a smile.

'Well, we'd better be off then. *Au revoir, Madame!*' they called as they scuttled away down the hill again through the vines and headed off towards the village school.

When I reached the Fennecs' house, it was Angèle who came out to greet me.

'Mother's having a day in bed; she's not feeling all that good. She wondered if you could possibly organize lunch for the boys when they come home. I'm not much good in the kitchen and father is up there with her and doesn't want to leave her. In any case, his cooking is different and the boys aren't that keen!'

I had never heard Angèle talk so much in all the months I had known her.

'Should I fetch the doctor, do you think?' I asked.

'Oh, I don't think so. Doctors cost money and she would have asked if she'd wanted one.'

So I set about finding my way round their kitchen, picked some green beans from the garden, a lettuce, and a small basket of tomatoes. There were onions hanging in strings in the barn, and herbs growing by the kitchen door. Angèle showed me where the spaghetti was, and as the boys got back at five minutes past twelve, lunch was on the table.

I wondered about Monique's lunch, and whether Louis would come down for some, but no one appeared, and Angèle said we had better not disturb them: they would ask if they wanted anything, she assured me.

The boys went back to school, and Angèle and I did the dishes and tidied everything up. What about supper, I asked. Supposing Monique was no better, perhaps I had better plan to do an evening meal as well. But Angèle said there was lots of soup from the day before, and they would have bread and cheese, as they usually did in the evenings.

As Angèle was busy doing something in the garden, and no one had emerged from upstairs, by half past two I had begun to wonder what I was doing there, when Louis suddenly appeared at the top of the stairs and called for me to come up.

Fearing some emergency, I entered the bedroom on tiptoe, to be greeted by Monique, sitting on the edge of the bed wreathed in smiles.

'I just wanted to thank you for holding the fort. It was very kind of you to come at a moment's notice, and I'm sure the boys had an excellent meal. There wouldn't be any of it left, would there?' she asked with a grin. 'I'm absolutely ravenous. And so must you be, Louis. You've had nothing since this morning, and we woke up at five.'

'I did ask Angèle if she thought you would wany anything,' I explained, 'but she said you were not to be disturbed. There is some left: I'll go and warm it up. I'm so glad you are feeling better.'

It was then that I caught sight of a tiny, swaddled bundle beside Monique on the bed. She did not give me time to say anything, but picked it up and announced:

'Meet our new daughter. Angèle will be pleased to have a sister. She's perfect, absolutely perfect. Louis is a very good midwife. We must remember, by the way, darling, to register her to-day or tomorrow at the latest at the *Mairie*. I hope no one cuts up nasty about our not having declared the pregnancy. After all, I don't see why you should have to if you don't want to tell anyone, do you?' she added, turning towards me.

'But then you lose those generous maternity allowances, don't you? And didn't you have any check-ups at all? I must say, I hadn't the slightest idea you were pregnant. Did no one know, except you and Louis?'

'No one. I never tell anyone. Blow their allowances! It's my business!'

'And I thought you were really ill! You could have knocked me over with a feather! Supposing there had been something wrong, though, wasn't it a big risk to take?'

'My dear,' Monique replied, 'if there had been anything wrong, I would have dealt with it, not some po-faced interfering doctor. A perfect baby, OK. Anything wrong ...' she looked me straight in the eye and I watched in horror as her powerful hands gave a determined twist to the imaginary dishcloth she seemed to be wringing out.

'By the way,' she added, 'don't tell people about the baby, will you. They only gossip behind one's back. And thanks for helping.

I shall be back on deck tomorrow.'

During the Christmas holidays the Fennecs sold their house at a handsome profit to an English couple, and moved away to yet another part of France. I must admit that I was not altogether sorry to see them go, though surprised that they never told me they were going. And, of course, I never heard where they went nor what became of them.

XVII   Family Photographs

I decided that I should try to get out a bit more. The idea of more bourgeois soirées alarmed me somewhat, even though I well realized that they were not all of the kind the vet was in the habit of organizing. And in any case, I was not at all sure that I felt at ease with the *petite bourgeoisie* of small French towns.

So when someone told me that a local choir was giving a concert in our church, I went along and thoroughly enjoyed the evening. On the whole, I fear, the French are not a musical nation, but this is largely because nothing is done to teach music in schools. It is simply not regarded as an academic subject and, like art, is just not taken seriously.

But I was quite impressed by the visiting choir and their conductor, and when I heard that they were based in a small country town only about thirty kilometres away, I decided to ask if I could join them. I had sung for many years in an excellent choir when I lived in England, read music at sight and knew a lot of the choral repertoire just about by heart. My application to join was accepted and I began to attend our weekly choir practices every Monday evening.

I very soon made friends with the delightful woman who sat next to me on our long, rather uncomfortable benches. And bit by bit I heard something about her life, a life that radiated love, generosity and self-sacrifice, though she would be the first to protest that she was no different from anyone else. But I thought she was very special.

'That's me,' said Marie-Elisabeth with a laugh, pointing to herself on the family photo she had brought along to show me that evening.

We were still sitting on our bench after the choir practice, having our usual ten minute chat. Lise, as she had always been called, lived in the town where the choir practices were held, about thirty kilometres from me, and as she was kept very busy with her many family commitments, we usually only met once a week during the singing season, which corresponds roughly with the school year, and at the concerts we gave occasionally, though we were mostly too busy to talk much then. But those weekly ten minutes had been enough, over the years, for me to get to know her well, and she came to treat me, as she said, 'like another sister'.

'I don't suppose you'd have recognized me; this was taken years ago, when Thomas – that's my second-from-the-youngest brother (that one there) had his twentieth birthday party, just before going off to do his military service. You see, we were all there, all twelve of us, can you imagine it? There's my older sister Marie-Madeleine, me, then Marie-Jeanne, then the oldest of the boys, Joseph, and René-Pierre, Matthieu and Michel. That's my third sister, Marie-Christine, who came after Michel, and then François, Simon and Thomas just before Bernard, the last. Quite a family it was: just imagine sitting down fourteen to meals every day! I don't know how my mother managed.'

She went on: 'We had to work terribly hard, not only helping with the younger children but working in the fields as well with our father. He was only a *métayer*, you know, not much more than a glorified farm labourer. Not his own land. Things were really hard then, not the way they are nowadays. But we managed somehow, and have always been a happy family. You can see that, can't you, from the photo? Nothing like living through hard times together to make you appreciate things, is there? Though I think some of the outdoor work was too much for a girl as young as I was; maybe that's why I had trouble with my back later. But that's life for you, isn't it? I've been very lucky, really.' She smiled, a gentle smile that glowed in her eyes; decades of patience and love so selflessly offered to her family and friends.

Her brothers and sisters could by then scarcely be said to resemble the tiny tots Lise had described to me: babies to be washed and changed, toddlers to be fed, played with and minded. Small children to help with their reading. And always endless washing to be done – no washing machine was known in their family until they had all grown up – so it was knuckle-scraping, hand-roughening work on a scrubbing-board, with a huge cake of

Savon de Marseille, outside in all weathers over a shallow stone sink let into the top of the thick wall that edged the veranda, where the waste water, drawn from the well, spilled out after use through three inches of pipe aimed directly at the flower bed below, and people would stop to wonder at the incredible hydrangeas that always seemed to thrive there, when their own were shrivelled and wasting in the intense heat of the summer months.

Now these young charges of Lise's were all grown-up. Some of the boys were clean-shaven; others sported beards, some neatly trimmed, some like vast encompassing curtains. Something for all tastes. They nearly all looked like scrum-halves in their Sunday best, though: broad-shouldered, strong young men (and some of them no longer all that young); a cheerful, pleasant team. The girls were all equally smartly dressed and happy-looking as befitted a Sunday family get-together. Clearly, Lise had done a good job of bringing up 'her' brood and was proud of them, though she missed the babies they had once been.

Our conductor was anxious to close up the hall, so Lise put her photo back into her handbag, kissed me first on the right cheek, then on the left, then on the right again, with a special, affectionate hug, before we drove off in opposite directions.

Her sister Marie-Madeleine, Mady, a year older than herself, had been the first to marry, and in due course had a little boy. Then Lise met Didier, a dashing young man who played the saxophone in a local band and travelled as a salesman for a multinational pharmaceutical company. They married when her sister was expecting her second child, and hoped that soon they would be able to announce a cousin for Mady's children.

Lise adored her Didier. They both longed for a child, 'to make us', as he would say, 'a proper family'. But as the years went by, and nothing happened, she began to realize that she would have to make do with her ever increasing numbers of nephews and nieces. But it hurt her to feel that she, of all the twelve, was incapable of bearing a child of her own, when so much of her young life had been spent looking after her small brothers and sisters. It was hard.

She tried never to show her disappointment and not to envy her siblings. She must live life as it came; she had Didier, after all.

Around the tenth anniversary of their wedding, she hurt her back – it had long shown signs of weakness – and was laid up for several months. All the family rallied round and did what they could to help, and Didier did as much as his busy schedules allowed, but during her illness Lise felt strangely cut off from the outside world, as if certain bonds had been broken, certain anchors lifted, leaving her adrift in an unfamiliar place.

Then one day, when her back was more or less better and she had resumed her household duties as well as she could, Didier, her Didier, told her about his affair. It wasn't, it never had been, a very serious affair, he assured her, but Yvonne (whose very existence was unknown to Lise) was expecting his child.

Lise had an egg in her hand when he spoke. Her stomach gave a lurch and everything inside her seemed suddenly to turn over. A sick, empty pain gripped her from her throat to her bowels. The egg slipped from her grasp onto the tiled floor and exploded over her feet, spattering Didier's trouser legs and shoes. In a supreme effort, she steadied herself and said: 'Oh, I'm so sorry, Didier. Just a moment, don't move! I'll clear it all up. Don't worry, just step out of the mess and I'll get it off your shoes, then you can change your trousers and I'll have them dry-cleaned.'

The activity made her feel less sick, and by the time Didier returned, carrying the stained trousers, she had taken her decision.

The few friends she told were unanimous. 'You must leave him, of course! Divorce him! You'll get everything, you know. It's the only way! How could you go on living with a man who'd do that to you? And why on earth doesn't she have an abortion, anyway? How can you stand the idea of him creeping off to see his child in her house? And her! And in the same town, too! What would people say? Oh, Lise, my dear, you couldn't live like that!'

But she did. She told Didier that he must recognize the child as his, and provide what was needed to bring it up. She intended to remain his wife, would continue to love him as before, and she rejoiced for him that at least he had this child, since she had been unable to give him one.

Time passed and the baby grew into a little boy, living with his mother but frequently visited by his father who, not unnaturally, adored him.

After a while, when she could bear her sense of isolation no longer, Lise suggested to Didier that Yvonne might care to bring young Pierrot over to tea one day. She could hardly wait till she saw him: such a lovely little man, a real poppet, enchanting, adorable, *un amour de petit bonhomme*, as wonderful as anything she could ever have imagined. She had bought games and toys to amuse him: they were for when he came with his Mummy to see her and his Daddy. She wanted to hug him to her, to cover him with kisses. But she simply sat smiling at the little lad, who smiled back, she thought, almost as if he understood.

Pierrot must have been about sixteen when Lise first told me about him. I was deeply moved by her story, so simple and natural it all seemed to her. She was so calm and sensible about it all. So French, one might have been tempted to say, but there was more to it than that. 'What's the point of being otherwise?' she asked me, with her usual sweet smile. 'After all, he's Didier's son, and so of course he's very close to me. Didier simply worships him. Teaching him the clarinet now, he is. Says he's not bad for a beginner; in fact he's doing very well at it.'

That summer Didier and Lise took young Pierrot and his mother on holiday with them to Châtelaillon Plage, to the north of Royan. Lise was full of it when we met again in early September. 'We had a really nice time, in spite of the few misgivings I felt beforehand. But everyone behaved with tact and consideration: no one trod on anyone's toes, if you see what I mean. And of course it gave me time to get to know Pierrot much better, though I was a bit upset at the way she would always answer any questions I asked him when we were all together. A bit steep, when the lad is sixteen, after all. But a wonderful thing happened one day when Pierrot and I met by accident as we were walking along the beach. He suddenly said: "You know, Lise" (that's what he calls me) "You know, when I'm eighteen, I'm going to get my driving licence, then I can come over to see you on my own whenever I like!" What do you think of that?'

Lise was ecstatic. She loved the boy almost as if he had been her own, for he was, after all, Didier's child, and she and Didier would have had children had God wanted them to. 'But that's life for you; we can't always arrange things as we think fit, can we?' she concluded as we made our way back to our respective cars, kissed one another good-night and went our separate ways until the following week.

'Didier seems to be in a state about his work.' Lise told me some time later. She was visibly anxious. 'He's not himself at all, but he doesn't want to talk about it, and I feel powerless to help. He says he can't concentrate and his work is getting on top of him. Not long ago they began asking the reps if they were willing to participate in some experiments, some kind of medical tests. They needed a large number of men of varying ages, and thought that they would get a fairly representative random sample among their own employees. But I can't say I know much about it, except that it involved some kind of bonus from the firm, and very little work, he said. Didier assured me there was no kind of risk whatever, so we left it at that. I'm not even sure whether the tests have taken place yet or not. But he seems unhappy and agitated and I don't know what to do. He's going to see the doctor next week: I hope he can do something to help.'

The doctor helped as best he knew how: with tranquillizers and sleeping pills and a recommendation to come back again in a week or two. Lise did not see much improvement, and the prescribed drugs, rather than returning Didier to his former cheerful, active self, seemed to have turned him into a kind of zombie, with whom Lise found all communication impossible. She was very anxious.

'I think he's been overworking for a long time, but what can one do? You see, he is head of his area, which is vast, and responsible for all the other reps, and this is simply added to all he had to do before. But with things as they are, you have to accept extra work. You can't refuse anything: it's all too easy to find yourself without a job at all. And we are so lucky that he is so highly thought of in the firm. Then of course, he plays with his group about four evenings a week, and that means very little sleep, as these things go on till all hours. But he loves playing; he wouldn't cut down on that for anything. At least not until this thing hit him. I wish I knew what caused depression, since I suppose that's what you'd call it.'

Didier and Lise celebrated their sixtieth birthdays in the same week, and of course a huge family get-together was planned. All the brothers and sisters were there, with their spouses and the thirty children they had produced between them over the years. Lise's mother, a wiry, agile eighty-two, was heard to say she wondered how they would have managed to accommodate them all if each of her children had spawned as many as she had! By now the obligatory family photograph posed quite a problem: ordinary cameras were not made to cope with such numbers. There were fifty-five closely packed faces to identify when Lise brought the photo to show me. Yes, they had had a good day together, but Didier seemed as depressed as ever.

Then the unthinkable happened. Alone in his own house one Saturday morning when Lise had gone to do the shopping at the local market, Didier shot himself through the head.

Ambulance, doctor, hospital; his inert body was examined and pronounced still living, but with what hope? No one dared say, and Lise could only hold his unconscious hand and offer up garbled prayers for his recovery.

Lise came to choir practice on the following Monday as usual: she could not bear just to sit at home alone, waiting, and there seemed little point in travelling a long way to the hospital every day just to look at her husband wrapped like a mummy and apparently just as lifeless. Though there was a ray of hope, they told her. Almost miraculously, they said, the bullet seemed to have missed anything vital. He might recover, even be his old self again. Time alone would tell.

'But the shock must have been terrible, my poor Lise!' I said, when she told me how she had found him lying in a pool of blood in his workshop, with their little dog nudging him and whining pathetically.

'Yes, it was not something I had ever thought he would do.' Lise went on: 'And of course, I had to tell Pierrot and his mother. That was almost the worst moment of my life. How can you explain, how can you tell a bright-eyed boy that his father didn't want to go on living? He just stood there and cried like a baby, once what I said had sunk in. It's going to be terrible for him: he is very close to Didier, you know. Very close.... She was upset too, you can imagine, but not quite as I would have expected. Somehow strange, she is. But I know it's easy for me to read things into people's behaviour, and I should just accept that people do react to things in different ways, don't they? How I sometimes wish life was straightforward, that people said what they meant and always told the truth. But maybe you think I'm just talking nonsense, and what has it got to do with all this, anyway? I wish I could explain, because I think you would understand.'

'Did Didier leave a note, or anything?' I asked.

'No, nothing. At any rate, nothing obvious. Of course, we all knew he was terribly depressed, but he didn't seem able to talk about it. But I do know it was not simply a 'cry for help', as some attempted suicides are. When you fire a gun into your own head, you mean it. You really mean it. That's what is so hard to take: that he would not talk to me about what was on his mind, that he felt he couldn't. Even if he recovers from this, I don't know whether he will ever explain. But you know, having you to talk to helps me enormously,' she added, 'I feel I can tell you things exactly as they are. It's a real help, especially at a time like this. I'll ring you during the week to let you know how things are getting on.'

Didier seemed to recover rapidly once he had regained consciousness. He spent a further fortnight in hospital undergoing all kinds of tests, then the neurologist told Lise that he could go home, provided she felt she could look after him. Somehow, goodness knows how, the bullet had missed all the vital centres of the brain: he could walk, talk and appeared to understand what was being said to him. He could read, remember what he had read, and write. He might even be able to drive again. It was possible, however, that his memory of the past was slightly impaired, the surgeon said, but only time would tell that with any certainty. It was early days yet, very early days, and the fact that he was alive was nothing short of a miracle.

Lise brought him home on the Sunday, just three weeks after the 'accident'. How else could she talk about that fatal day? She could hardly avoid referring to the event, but could not bring herself to say 'the day you tried to commit suicide' or 'the day you shot yourself' to Didier himself. She knew, and so did all her friends and family, what had in fact happened, but she began to wonder whether perhaps Didier was not very clear in his own mind about what he had done, and thought it better not to elicit questions that risked bringing back memories too painful to bear for the time being.

The hospital sent him home with the usual letters for his doctor and all the X-rays and scans they had taken during his stay, for here in France the patient is the guardian of his own medical records. Lise was not one to leave such things lying around, so she found a home for them in the 'medical' section of their large filing cabinet, just beyond the most recent inclusion, a small envelope she did not remember seeing before. Thinking that something had perhaps been misplaced, she gave a quick glance at the contents. A brief letter and the kind of form laboratories use for analyses of various kinds. Something to do with Didier's work, to judge from the heading. They thanked him for his willingness to participate in testing the revolutionary new spermicide they were working on, but in view of the results of the enclosed sperm count, there seemed little point, in his case, of bothering him any further. And a scribbled signature that meant nothing to her.

One glance at the form confirmed what the letter had already told her. Didier's live sperm count was virtually nil. He was infertile. He must always have been infertile. She couldn't bear it. And Pierrot, what about Pierrot, her darling Pierrot? Was he to be taken from her, too, along with all the children she might have had, if things had been different, but now knew she never would?

She put the letter and the form back into their envelope and hid it in her bag.

Little by little she came to the conclusion that Didier had forgotton certain things, a notion reinforced when he asked to see his son. Pierrot came over for the afternoon and played the clarinet, to Didier's great delight. They were like two children together, laughing and joking as they wolfed an entire box of chocolate biscuits.

After Pierrot had gone, she went and made a light supper for Didier and herself, which they ate together by the fire, as the evenings were chilly, and it seemed more like home to light the fire for his first evening back with her. He appeared quite cheerful and talked of this and that, mostly his time in hospital (the part he could remember, though she was not clear about whether he realized he had been unconscious for several days).

Later, after Lise had got Didier ready for bed (for she had to do just about everything for him) she sat alone for a few minutes looking at the dying embers. Then she took the letter from her handbag and put it on the fire. As the paper burned blue among the last of the logs, she thought of all the things she should be grateful for.

'Yes, I'm managing all right, now,' she replied to my anxious questions at the next rehearsal. 'Didier's fine. He needs a lot of help, of course. You see,' she confided, her voice dropping almost to a whisper, 'he's just like a child, you know. Just like a child.'

I am glad to be able to say that Didier is making great progress and is more or less independent again, though he had to retire, of course, from his job. Young Pierrot has a job now, but he hasn't forgotten his clarinet and occasionally joins Didier on one of the group's musical evenings. And as for Lise, she never complains, although her back is giving her trouble again, I fear. Perhaps it is not surprising after all she has had to cope with.

Then I met another person who has had a lot to cope with, although the circumstances were by no means similar. It was when I began to look at some houses on behalf of the friends who gave me my first two hens. Their children were growing up and they were really keen to find a place of their own. So, having undertaken to look at what the market had to offer, I was sent to see all sorts of places through various agencies. Only about one in ten of the houses I saw bore the slightest resemblance to what I thought they might have in mind, while the other nine were totally unsuitable, some outrageously so.

I was still passionately attached to my own house, and went home to it from wherever I had been with a feeling of joyous excitement and ever-renewed delight. But I could see possible difficulties looming on the horizon, for my neighbour Fernando, now Helen had turned her back on him, was beginning to look with suspicious interest in my direction, and although nothing had been said, I feared the possibility of being required some day to declare myself friend or foe. As foe, my life could have been made very difficult, and I was not at all sure whether I could trust him as friend. So the idea that I might, one day, have to consider moving, was sadly beginning to be a real, even if distant possibility.

It was when I went on one of these house-viewing excursions that I met a family – father, mother and daughter – living in the most primitive conditions I have ever seen. And although I knew from the outset that their house was of no possible interest, either to my friends or to me, they insisted that I see all over it. People are like that down here, and one does not want to offend them.

It was a huge place, although they appeared to camp in three small rooms: three rooms that reeked of decades of neglect. There was no proper bedding on the beds, just a pile of dirty old blankets, while such clothes as they possessed, apart from what they were wearing, hung on hooks behind each door. I thought of Granny Boniface's sparkling floors and windows, and reflected on how vital a role women play as homemakers in this rural society. It rapidly became obvious that in this household the wife had opted for the escape route of alcoholism. But her husband and daughter Emilia struggled on, each attempting in their own way to obtain some satisfaction from their lives.

XVIII   The Cardigan

It was the most beautiful cardigan Emilia had ever seen, and wrapped with such care that she had scarcely dared open the plastic bag and touch the fine, white angora wool. But her English neighbour – she never could pronounce her name, *'L'Anglaise'*, anyway, that would do – she stood over her expecting her to undo it, even try it on. There was no way she would put this virginal garment over her dirty work-a-day clothes. It had to be kept for a very special occasion. A wedding, perhaps, or New Year's Eve, the night of the Saint Sylvestre.

She stared myopically through the bag at the delicate, lace-like knitted fabric, holding it close to her eyes, one of which was swollen and ringed with black, and wondered how anything so fine could ever have been made. And so soft.... It was like the down of a newly hatched chick, or the fur of those tiny kittens her father had told her to drown last week. That cat was always having kittens, but she had never had any as pretty as those before. Long, soft fur, they had, by the time their crafty mother had brought them back to the house, already tussling with one another and leaping into the air after the flies that hung permanently around the farmyard.

She had once had down, too, on her upper lip, but by now it was beginning to look like her mother's, thicker and blacker with every day that passed, and when she touched it, it felt scratchy sometimes. How had her mother ever managed to get herself a husband with a moustache like that, she wondered.

Then she caught sight of her finger, the one that was stroking the cardigan, and saw how black and rough it looked beside the fine white wool. Her nails were broken and lined with earth – what could you expect with the life she led? Looking after the vegetables, mucking-out the cows twice a day, heaving bales of hay down from the loft above the cow-stalls and lifting them into each stall, feeding and cleaning out the hens, the ducks, the geese, the rabbits.

That was another world, the rabbits. They sometimes had fur like the cardigan, particularly the babies from the mother in the furthest cage to the left, the one nearest the well. Not when they were first born, of course. They were completely naked for several days, eyes closed and all, like kittens, and you were not supposed to look at them then, in case the mother ate them. So she kept an old sack over the cage once she saw the mother begin to assemble her nest, busily heaping up straw to form a mound in the darkest corner of the cage.

They always seemed to have their babies in the night, and the following morning you would find the mother sitting beside the mound of straw as if nothing had happened, but if you looked very carefully you could see a scrap of white fur sticking out of the very middle of the mound. She pulled the white fur from her own tummy to line the nest and it was so soft, so soft. Then you knew the babies had arrived. Sometimes as many as ten. She could just cope with ten, the mother could: she had ten teats. But more than ten usually meant that the weakest got no food.

Not like calves they were. She had only once seen twin calves born, and they had had to call the vet for that. Oh, yes, and when that large calf had to be pulled out by its back legs with a rope round its hooves. Just got up straight away and teetered over to its mother, it did. Sort of ready-made, cows seemed to be. Nice gentle cows they were, she thought, these *Blondes d'Aquitaine*, with their pale hides the colour of milky coffee. When her father punched her she would always pretend one of the cows had kicked her in the eye. Luckily they didn't have many callers, living as isolated as they did. The *Anglais* had bought the house opposite because it was the back of beyond. They liked it that way. But they weren't there very often, so they didn't realize how often he punched her.

She sometimes wondered why he didn't punch her mother too, because she really was a slob. Never did anything, and when she and her father came in from the fields, there were the dishes unwashed, no food ready, and her mother slouched over the table, drunk. They had to re-kindle the fire, take down some dry sausage from the rack over the fireplace, fetch wine from the *chai*, grab a couple of glasses from the sink and use their pocket-knives to cut themselves slices of sausage, which they ate with huge hunks of bread from the big *pain de campagne* her father brought back twice a week from the town.

There was no hot water except what they boiled over the fire, and only the kitchen sink to wash in, so it was not surprising that her hands were always rough and dirty-looking.

'It's very kind of you. It's lovely,' she said to the neighbour, and blushed, so unused to speaking she was, and especially thanking anyone for anything, for there was so little in her life to be thankful for.

It was late February. In January the cat had had her kittens, as she usually did. The same would happen again in August. Now it was almost spring and the blossom was beginning to show: the wild cherry-plums and the flaming red spiky Japonica were already well out. Soon the apricots would be in bloom, followed by the plums, and woe betide the poor trees if frost caught them as the fruit was setting. While the cold weather held the vines back, she and her father must get them all pruned and clear away the prunings, collecting them up into faggots for kindling, each huge bundle tied with the same osiers they used to tie in the vine shoots. That was hard on the hands, because although they soaked the osiers overnight in cold water, by the end of the day the bundle they carried strapped to their waists under a wide belt would have more or less dried and become brittle and cut her fingers. It wasn't too bad a job if the sun shone, but no fun at all under a leaden sky, or worse, a bitter wind with volleys of sleet or even the occasional flurry of snow.

She remembered one year when it had really snowed. Her father had cursed and sworn because he could not get his tiny car out – one of those *voitures sans permis*, really a glorified moped with a flimsy body built around it. The thing couldn't go faster than thirty kilometres an hour. He had no driving licence, neither did she, nor her mother for that. Not that *she* would have been safe driving, pissed as she always was. You didn't, in fact, need a licence for her father's car, but there were limits all the same. No one ever drove it but her father.

The snow may have been a nuisance, but before the ducks had fouled it up it had been so beautiful. Just like her cardigan: pure white and sort of fluffy looking. She would find a hanger for it and hang it with her other things on the back of her bedroom door. Not that she had much: one skirt and her best dress, pretty old by now but still serviceable. And just as well, since she didn't know who would buy her another one when it fell to bits. The rest of her things she wore every day, so they didn't need to be hung. A very old, ill-fitting skirt, a pair of ancient trousers held up with string for when she worked with hay and straw, or when the weather was particularly cold, an old jumper and the jacket her father had handed down to her. At least that had large pockets for her secateurs and her knife, pockets into which she could occasionally thrust her hands to warm them for a few moments, until he shouted at her to get on.

She thought she understood *l'Anglaise* to say that they were on their way to Spain. To find the sun, she had said, pointing to the sky. Fancy only staying for one night, she thought, and wondered about where they went in Spain and how many houses they had around the world. They said *au revoir* to one another and, in spite of her black eye, Emilia's downy upper lip creased in a smile as she clutched the precious cardigan, still well protected by its plastic bag, to her filthy old jacket.

'I do hope she likes it,' said the neighbour to her husband, once back in their civilized modern kitchen. 'It's hard to tell with her. She seemed to have got another black eye from one of the cows. They must have it in for her. They always look so gentle to me, but I must be wrong. She could hardly see out of one eye tonight. And she's still wearing that impossible jacket of her father's. It stinks, it really does.'

'It's not to be wondered at,' her husband replied in his usual calm manner. 'She works so hard; her life is really tough, I think, with her mother more or less a dead weight in the family, and the brother busy with his own life. If you can call that a life,' he added, 'working on a conveyor belt in a bottling factory. But she does a man's work. Have you ever noticed her muscles, in the summer when her arms are bare?'

'No dear, I don't think I have. Well, anyway, I hope she likes the cardigan. It was one of M&S's, you know, so it should be all right. Now I'd better get our supper so we don't get late to bed. Have you put on the electric blankets, dear? I think the beds are always better for being thoroughly aired, don't you, dear?'

Emilia had deposited the cardigan on her unmade bed until she had time to arrange to hang it up. The bed had a large, square pillow, but as it had never known a pillow-case, it was decidedly grubby, as was the pile of miscellaneous blankets, some of which she lay on while the others served to cover her. She had never known anything else, though just occasionally had caught a glimpse of some magazine, probably in the doctor's waiting-room, with pictures of sheets: pretty floral sheets, or even snow-white ones, sometimes embroidered. You had to be pretty rich to have white sheets. Whatever would become of them in their family, living as they did, she wondered.

She clattered down the stairs and out through the kitchen to muck out and feed the cows. It was beginning to get dark and she was late with her work. Tomorrow she would be in the vines all day, after doing the cows, the rabbits, hens, ducks and geese, and when they came home it would be cows, rabbits, hens, ducks and geese all over again. Not to mention doing something for the three of them to eat. She thought about the cardigan, and it warmed her heart.

In the morning she was up well before dawn, though she noticed how the days were lengthening. She washed her face and hands at the sink, then peeled some vegetables and put them on to boil to make their soup for later on. She made some coffee for her parents and drank a big bowlful mixed with some creamy milk she had got from Gertrude the evening before, as her calf didn't seem to get through it all: he was still rather small. Then, while the soup was simmering, she went out to open up the hens, clean out their house, and throw them their morning grain. After that it was up to them to scratch away in the yard until nightfall, when she would have to lock them up again for fear of the fox.

Perhaps that was how her father thought of her: a prize hen to be locked up at night for fear of the fox. She had heard people say that all Italian fathers (and mothers, though hers didn't count) locked their daughters up until they were married. A question of family honour, it would seem. Anyway her family was no exception, although she had ways and means of outwitting him when she wanted to: she wasn't his daughter for nothing, the cunning old fox he was. After all, she was nearly thirty now, she was entitled to a bit of freedom, though she kept her opinions strictly to herself. No need to go looking for black eyes, was there?

'You ready, then?' her father asked gruffly. It was the first time he had spoken that morning and she knew he would be away a moment later. She took the soup off the boil, flung their three bowls into the sink and ran a thin stream of cold water over them, put a cloth over the bread, made sure her knife and secateurs were in her pocket, and, shouting good-bye to her mother, ran after him, catching him up as he strode across the yard, past the big oak and down the steep track that led to their four fields and the vines beyond.

The sun had begun to shine after a fortnight's rainy weather. Always was a change in the weather around the full moon, she thought, and that was tonight. There was a feel of spring in the air. The cold winds had gone and the lightest of breezes blew almost warm on her face as she made her way slowly and deliberately along the rows of bare vines, cutting out all the luxuriant growth of the previous year, to leave nothing but a bare skeleton: one stubby branch with two buds on it and one long, curving branch to be tied like an arch onto the taut parallel wires that held the vines. But they would not start the tying-in until all the pruning was done, so her fingers would be spared for a few days yet.

She rather liked working in the vines. It was quiet, not like driving their wretched, smelly tractor, or sitting with her mother, perched on those uncomfortable little metal seats behind her father, operating the drill that planted maize seeds one by one, or rather two by two, since she usually managed to get her mother to pull her lever at the right moment, just as she pulled hers, so that the lines would germinate nice and straight. And her father clucking like a gruff old hen at them from his seat on the tractor.

The vines ... no, she mustn't think about that now. They were her secret place. The only pleasure she had in life. If her father knew! He would kill her, she felt sure. But now she had to work and not think about that. That would be later, after everyone had gone to bed, and the full moon shone white across the fields, and she would run the way she had walked this morning, the way she would return for a bowl of soup with lots of bread in it, the way she would come back again in the afternoon, and return home, exhausted, for the cows, the hens, the rabbits. Then supper, and the remaining chores. Sometimes there was a hen to kill and pluck, or a rabbit to skin. And of course her father needed help with the tractor more often than not, and that meant lying on the ground on her back under the beastly smelly thing, nearly tearing her guts out as she tugged at this bit or that, while her father swore at her in Italian.

She knew French better than her parents did, since she had been to school here in France. So when Mario, her brother, dropped in with friends from work on a Sunday, she talked French to them and her parents found it hard to follow. It gave her a feeling of independence to talk to these young men in their own language, which they told her she spoke just like them. They would smile and say nice things to her that made her feel good. One of them had once – oh! years ago, when she was about twenty – asked her if she ever walked among the vines or along the avenues of maize of an evening. He thought it was fun to find yourself completely lost in rows of maize eight feet high, in what had been a small, familiar field before the crop had begun to grow. And of course, no one had the slightest idea that anyone was there!

And that was how she learnt to outmanoeuvre the old fox. And that was when he started to punch her. Perhaps he sensed he was being circumvented, but she was more cunning even than he, and what did a few black eyes matter when she had her secret independence, her private defiance of him, her moonlit walks with one or other of her brother's pals.

Of course her brother didn't know anything about all this. He might well have sprung to the defence of the family. It was her secret, and no one would ever know.

It was Gérard who came that evening. The full moon made him passionate, as it did her, and they lost no time in small-talk. It was too wet after all the rain to lie down among the vines, so he turned her round, threw her skirt up over her shoulders, pulled her pants down round her knees, as she bent almost double in an ecstasy of expectation, feeling his warm flesh against her buttocks, waiting for him to penetrate her. She liked it like this: it was animal, basic, and deeply satisfying.

The cares of the day with all its hard work, her father's carping criticism of everything she did, her mother's bibulous incompetence, all faded into oblivion when she did this. She was liberated, free to be herself. It was the one thing in her life that made all the rest tolerable.

A few weeks later, round about mid-March, her father produced an invitation to a cousin's wedding. Like a good Italian father, he brought in the post and read it to the family, regardless of the name on the envelope. He told the two women that they would all be going, as it was not too far away. He thought that they might, at a pinch, all get into the little car, though they would have to drive even more slowly because of the added weight. He would look for a suitable present for the cousin and his bride.

The cardigan, she thought. Yes, it would not be too hot in April, just perfect. The wedding was to be just after Easter, which fell early in the month that year. It would look good over her 'best' dress and would hide the most faded parts. What an occasion! She had not been to a wedding since she was a child, and she knew that grown-ups had great fun at weddings. Perhaps she would meet someone who wanted to marry her, you never knew what might happen at a wedding.

They reached the church where the wedding mass was being celebrated just as the bride and groom emerged from the civil ceremony in the *Mairie* and processed across the square before the entire village population and the many guests from outside who had gathered there to throw their handful of rice and bags of confetti. Then everyone squeezed into the church as best they could. The nuptial blessing was given and the mass was said. More confetti and rice was thrown, and the jollity began: an enormous and very vinous lunch in the best local restaurant, attended by at least a hundred and fifty people, a lunch that lasted till five o'clock in the afternoon, followed by an *apértif* for those who had not been invited to the first meal (and those who had, she noticed) this being followed by another, even grander meal, including dancing in the open air under an awning the restaurant erected for such occasions.

The new fluffy white cardigan made Emilia feel like a queen. Never had she worn anything so gloriously soft, so sparkling white. She looked like a blushing bride herself, strangely innocent and youthful amidst this motley crowd of relatives and friends of the bride and groom. This was her day, the greatest event of her life. White tablecloths, food such as she had never eaten, glasses that must surely be crystal, music, dancing ... and then suddenly she saw him.

She felt her heart contract. She gasped. He was looking at her. He was coming over to where she stood, smiling at her. As she spoke she felt desire for him rise like a tide, a tide that swept everything else away. Here, she thought, was someone so wonderful, so incredible, that he would not need to be kept secret. She went out into the night with him, down towards the little river that ran through the village, until the sounds of the meal and the dancing had dimmed, and they could talk to one another in whispers as they sat on the river bank.

She did not remember very clearly what they had talked about, but she did remember how gentle he was, how he took her face between his hands, and kissed her eyes, the tip of her nose, her ears, her neck. How he stroked her hair, her throat, then, tucking one finger between two buttonholes, ran it round the contours of her firm, bare breasts, round and round, round and round, until she began to moan. Then he began to kiss her mouth, exploring its depths with his tongue, and slowly undid the buttons of her white cardigan, then those of the dress beneath it, so that he could bring his head down lower and kiss the hard nipples.

She remembered that he had taken off his own jacket and laid it on the ground, so that her white cardigan would not suffer. After that he explored more and more of her body, stroking her belly, teasing the innermost part of her thighs with a practised finger, giving her unimagined pleasure. She could not remember exactly how they had finished, but the explosion of her pent-up desire was something she would never be able to forget.

They lay on the bank for a while afterwards, until he said, gently stroking her face, that perhaps they should think of rejoining the party in case their absence had been noticed. She thought of the fox, and laughed.

Back at home, her father never asked her where she had been, nor indeed whether she had enjoyed herself. She began to realize how little he spoke to her about anything. It was all orders, complaints or black eyes. She got two of those on their first day back. If only she could get a job in the bottling factory where her brother worked, she would be shot of the farm. She must think about that. Unless, of course, *he* were to turn up one day and whisk her away on a white horse to his castle. Then she remembered that she didn't even know his name.

A day or so later, she discovered that her white cardigan was missing from the back of her door. She had noticed that, in spite of all the precautions taken, it showed signs of having been on the ground: the back was slightly muddy and two grass-stains had spoiled its vestal whiteness. Try as she might, with a damp rag smuggled up from the kitchen, the stains remained, indeed got worse the more she rubbed. In the end she had decided to put it away in its bag and hang it in the usual place until she could think what best to do to get it clean again.

But someone had come into her room and removed the cardigan, bag and all. She asked her mother, who muttered something like 'Ask him!' So, feeling she had nothing to lose, she challenged her father.

'Was it you who took my cardigan?'

No reply.

'Father, I'm asking you something, and I want an answer. Did you take my white cardigan from the door in my room, and if you did, what have you done with it?'

Her father turned and looked at her, inscrutable.

'Unless you tell me what you've done with it, I'm leaving here and going to work in the bottle factory with Mario.'

He had not expected this and began to rub his chin, a sign that he didn't quite know what to say.

'What makes you think they'd employ a whore like you, may I ask?'

'Tell me where my cardigan is!' she screamed at him.

'All right then. I'll tell you. I reckoned you wouldn't be wanting it any more, now it's all dirty, so I've put it down the well.'

She gasped.

'You don't seem to realize that I'm nearly thirty and that I want a life of my own! Don't you care? What sort of a man are you, anyway?' she flung at him as she turned on her heel in fury.

Summer followed upon spring, and Emilia remained at home. Jobs at the bottle factory were much sought after, her brother told her. And in any case, where would she live?

Since the wedding, she had not been down among the vines or the maize at night. Somehow, she didn't feel she wanted to any more, and feared provoking her father any further for the time being. A kind of uneasy truce reigned between them: he feared being left to manage the farm on his own, which he clearly could not do, and seemed to have softened his attitude towards his daughter. Only a little, mind you, but enough for her to have noticed. She still felt furious beyond belief at the thought of her beloved white cardigan mouldering at the bottom of the well, but there was no point in making herself ill about it. He was just a barbarian, that was all there was to it.

Autumn came with the *vendange*: she and her father brought in the grapes, each bunch cut by hand with tiny sharp secateurs. The result of each day's work had to be pressed, and the deep trailer behind the tractor washed clean, ready for the next day's harvest. It was back-breaking work, and lasted the best part of two weeks. But it was a good year, and her father seemed pleased.

Then one day an extraordinary thing happened. A van drew up at the house, and a man got out carrying a tall white cylinder. He had come, he said, to bring them hot water. After much discussion and bustling here and there, it was agreed to install the thing where the man suggested, and half a day's work later, the sink had a second tap from which ran hot water, hotter than the hand could bear.

Her father's only comment was that it would be easier to keep the place clean now. Life had indeed taken on a new dimension.

Christmas was celebrated by going to Midnight Mass at their local church, after which the family gathered for the *Réveillon*. Mario brought eight dozen oysters, traditional fare for this particular night. Then the children's father surprised them all by producing a large slab of *Foie Gras*, a freshly roasted chicken and a box full of pâtisseries from the best *pâtissier* in the nearby town. Such largesse was not customary, but no one asked any questions and they all made the most of this unexpected feast. Mario stayed what was left of the night, dossing down where he could, since the following day was Sunday, and the bottling plant did not open again until the Monday.

At about five in the morning Emilia woke with violent stomach cramps: oysters did this to people sometimes if they were not perfectly fresh. She got up and went to see whether Mario had been affected too, but found him deep asleep. There was no sign of activity from her parents' room either; in fact she could hear her mother snoring away as usual, while her father's breathing resembled more of a whistle than a snore. In any event, they were both sound asleep and clearly not troubled by the oysters. Her cramps had eased enough for her to wonder whether she had dreamt it all, then suddenly they began again, twisting her gut tighter and tighter, and she found herself holding on to the end of the bed, wondering if the pain would ever stop. When they began again ten mintues later, she waited till the worst was over and decided to wake Mario.

He was not easy to wake, and by the time he had realized that there was something wrong, Emilia began another spasm. He knew she had put on weight, but seeing her in her night-dress made him realize just how much, and he leapt out of bed and pulled on his clothes, urging her to do the same.

'Don't let's wake our parents, or they'll worry,' he said, now calm and efficient. 'But you, my girl, you should be in hospital, and that's where I'm going to take you right now. Mustn't play about with these things, you know. You need help.'

And he bundled her into his car and drove off to their local hospital. Her cramps continued during the journey, if anything growing more frequent, and Mario was glad to see the hospital gates and hand her over to someone more competent than he was.

Ten minutes later a nurse called him in to see his niece. The most beautiful baby in the world, Emilia thought, once she had got used to the idea that she was hers. She simply hadn't realized, she only knew about animals. People were different. She had had no idea.

The hospital saw no point in keeping a perfectly healthy mother and child in, especially between Christmas and New Year, and more particularly as they had not been booked in. So Mario drove them both back to the farm, where Emilia made the morning coffee and milked Babette, who had too much, so that she and her brother and their parents could have their coffee as they liked it in the mornings.

Her father was the first to come down.

'You're up early,' he remarked, surprised to see his son already dressed, and on Christmas morning, too.

Then he saw the baby. The tiny, fragile creature was asleep, her brow slightly puckered and her little fists clenched. Her skin had a bloom on it like a peach: soft and golden, overlaid with pink. All he said was 'Oh!' and went out in the direction of his workshop.

Within a minute he was back, carrying the most gorgeous Moses-basket Emilia had ever seen. Inside it was a delicate, white, knitted shawl and a baby blanket as soft as the fur on a mother-rabbit's tummy. And under the blanket, a tiny, tiny white cardigan, so soft, so soft …

'But father …' Emilia could find no words.

'It's my grandchild, isn't it?' He paused for a moment. 'Boy or girl?'

'She's a girl.'

'Then we shall call her Marie-Noëlle. And now, give me my coffee.'

Emilia's father decided not to sell the property in the end, and his little granddaughter roams happily amongst the hens, the ducks, the geese and even the cows who, being of a gentle disposition, never cause her the slightest harm. I occasionally see the old man out in his little *voiture sans permis*, but living as I do some distance away, I have not kept in touch as I might, had they been closer neighbours.

XIX   What's in a Name?

I did not have to live long in France to discover that what the British commonly consider to be a Christian name can, over here, often be a surname. You will find people called Raymond, Marcel, Henri, Paul, Jean, André, François – the list is almost endless – and not be quite sure at first if you are not committing some dreadful impropriety in calling them by what must surely be their first name. And this situation is further complicated by the fact that people are often addressed in writing as Monsieur Paul, Raymond, rather than as Monsieur Raymond Paul, thus adding to the confusion of the unfortunate foreigner.

So when Monsieur Roger introduced himself to me one fine summer morning as he stood beside his ancient black MGA in the car-park of the Hostellerie du Grand Carrefour (definitely the best hotel in the area), I was not sure whether I was using his surname or his first name in calling him Monsieur Roger.

The owner of the hotel, to whom I had mentioned that I might possibly be thinking of selling my house, had suggested I meet Monsieur Roger, who was staying in the hotel and hoping to find a suitable home in the area for his wife, himself and their three horses.

He was a charming man. He told me he was seventy-five, but I could only marvel at how well preserved he was: slim, elegant and well-groomed, dressed in a lightweight jacket and grey flannels, with a deep blue silk cravat at the open neck of his white shirt, he exuded the England that was, the England of before the last war, the England of the discreetly well-to-do, with their perfect manners and their beloved sports cars. Possibly an Englishman of his generation would not have chosen soap or talc (or was it aftershave?) with such a pronounced fragrance but, don't misunderstand me, it was in no way excessive and, being of the

174

highest quality, not at all unpleasant.

'Actually, I am Belgian,' he explained. 'I do speak English – not very well, but enough to get by – and I greatly admire the British and their way of life. As you see, my car is British. It's been my great friend for many years.'

I had noted the car, but, coming on it side-on, had not seen the red and white Belgian number-plates it carried.

'Where are you living at present?' I enquired, curious to situate this enigmatic person, who could well, as far as I was concerned, have flown in from Mars.

'My wife and I are in the Ariège at the moment. We have a big house, almost a château, I suppose one might call it, up in the mountains. But my wife has been finding the local people increasingly difficult to live with, and to tell the truth, I feel she needs a change of scene. I have a hunch she would like this area. You see, my wife is not an easy person to get on with. She has had what you might call a tragic life, and there are very few people she likes or trusts, which doesn't make things any easier for me, I must admit, but there you are.'

I was curious to know more, but only dared venture the most general of questions regarding his wife's health.

As he replied, it was as if a great abyss opened up in front of the summery car-park and I found myself whisked down into the dark ages of wartime Belgium when it had been overrun by the advancing Nazis and occupied by German troops and the dreaded Gestapo.

'I was in the Belgian resistance, of course, like most of the upper-class families in Brussels who more or less ran it all,' he explained. 'I was in charge of one section and had a number of helpers, whose business was mainly to feed us with information in the most discreet way possible. I suppose I was about thirty-five then, though isn't it difficult when you get older to remember how old one was at such-and-such a time?'

He paused, and I felt he had somehow changed gear, and was reliving a part of his life that had altered him profoundly, something he felt a need to confide in someone, in anyone willing to listen.

'Among our "intelligence" helpers were a couple of girls. Discreet and not particularly noticeable girls – about twenty or so, they must have been, though I think the younger one was only eighteen when they began to work for us. Very useful they were, too, until one of them got caught and handed over to the Gestapo. She was there three days before I realized what had happened, but when I heard, I broke into the headquarters – don't ask me how – and managed to get her out, though not before they had made the most terrible mess of her – I will spare you the details.'

He paused again, his gaze distant and troubled, before resuming his story. 'She lived in hiding till the end of the war, of course, and I somehow managed to survive and carry on the good work. But I felt a great sense of guilt at having allowed a young life like that girl's to be destroyed, since that was in effect what had happened to her. A broken body: she had a number of operations to repair what they had done to her. And above all a deranged mind. What would happen to her when her parents were no longer there to look after her? So you see, I married her, hoping that eventually she would feel secure and loved by someone who would not let her down ...'

'I see ...,' I murmured, deeply moved by his story. Of course there had to be things left unexplained in so brief a tale. One could hardly question him, though, only hope that a fuller picture would emerge in its own good time.

Then he seemed to change gear once again, and began to talk about his life with his parents before and during the war years, for he had remained a bachelor until his marriage to Béatrice. (At least she had a name now, something to attach a personality to. It helped me to visualize her, although when we eventually met, she was not at all what I had imagined!)

'I had always got on very well with my parents. We lived a quiet life and had common interests, somewhat intellectual, although one of our greatest pleasures was walking. Most week-ends we would drive into the Ardennes, leave the car and walk all day, taking a picnic lunch. It was my greatest joy: all those wonderful wild flowers, and the mountain views, the peace of it all – a real rest cure.'

'Unfortunately my wife did not like walking, at least, not with my parents. And she resented the little time I spent with them, although she lacked nothing, absolutely nothing. So that was a great sadness to me. When my father died a few years after my marriage, I felt I had betrayed him. He missed my companionship so much in those last years, and I had thought everything would go on as it had before. But what could I do?'

We set off to look over my house, which Monsieur Roger

thought entirely suitable for their needs, except for the fact that my mere acre of land would not be adequate for the three horses. Was there a nearby field that they could rent? He must fetch his wife to see the house, but not before certain problems had been overcome.

'Could we rent it from you, rather than buy it?' he asked. 'No, I'm afraid not,' I replied. 'You see, if I move, I shall have to buy another house, and will need the money. And in any case if I rented this one, I would have to pay capital gains tax on it when I eventually came to sell it.'

'It's so beautifully isolated. It's exactly what we need. But with the dollar falling lower every day – and that is where my money is – I had really hoped to be able to rent until my finances improved. And there's another thing. When I die, which will in all probability be before my wife, I have to make sure that she is properly provided for. But since we have no children and no remaining parents, everything she inherits from me will, when she dies, go to her sister, and that I could not agree to.'

Suddenly I felt drawn into his life with all its problems. The complete stranger I had met only that morning had made me his confidant, and, like it or not, I must help as best I could. Just why he was telling me all these things I did not ask myself, so sincere did he appear. The fact was I felt sorry for the man.

The following day he was to go and fetch his wife, if she agreed to come, he said. He did not like her being alone for too long, although she always carried a gun, he told me. The house was very isolated, but they had had a few problems with the local people, he added. And his wife had threatened to shoot anyone who approached the house.

'And she would, too,' he added. 'So I had better get back to her and not leave her on her own too long. If you would allow me to have your telephone number, I will let you know when I shall be back with her, and we can discuss the matter further. There must be some solution that would satisfy us all, don't you think?'

A week went by and I heard nothing more, then just when I had decided that they would not be coming, I received a call from the hotel, and was told that Monsieur and Madame Roger were in residence and would be pleased if I would meet them in the foyer the following morning at ten and accompany them back to my house to show them both over it.

Henri Roger greeted me warmly, clasping my hand between both of his as if renewing acquaintance with a long-lost friend. His wife Béatrice gave me a limp handshake, scarcely brushing my fingers with hers, as if preferring to remain isolated from human contact. In a flash she had scanned my face, my hands, my clothes, then taken refuge once again within herself.

As we approached the house down the kilometre of rough road that led to the large, square building with its huge walnut tree and surrounding fruit orchard, Béatrice began to show signs of agitation.

'*Mais où vais-je pouvoir mettre mes chevaux?*' she kept repeating, as if the only thing that mattered was where her horses were to go.

Her husband suggested that she should first see if she liked the house, then they would see what could be done to let the horses have more land to graze on. So we went in and I showed them around, or rather he did, for he had clearly fallen in love with the place and remembered every detail of what I had told him about it. I was amazed at his mental agility – no doubt he needed to keep his mind needle-sharp to be able to cope with her.

She decided that the main bedroom, which was huge by any standards, would be hers, although it was certainly not large enough to accommodate all her wardrobes, she said. So she appropriated the equally large study, which had been added in part of the barn, for her clothes, thus relegating her husband to a small back room next to the study in which, it seemed, he was to live, move and have his being, in other words sleep, read, write (and do the household accounts, he added wryly).

As for my kitchen, naturally it did not meet her standards. That would all have to be re-done, of course. And another bathroom added: she could not share a bathroom, having always, she said, had her own.

'If you saw our present house,' she confided, her mood somewhat less distant than when we had first met, 'you would realize how hard it is for me to leave it. A huge drawing-room, with a great high-domed ceiling hung with deep red velvet – I had that done, of course – and my bedroom with all my fitted wardrobes – they are all in solid rosewood, you know – I just don't know how they will even get in through the doors here, let alone fit any of the rooms!'

I had visions of her enormous château with splendid double

doors and panelling on every wall, and four or five luxurious bathrooms such as one saw on the television advertisements, where boy-slender, alluring women climb endless, totally unnecessary tiled steps up to a dais, there to disrobe, stretch their arms heavenward, and spray their armpits with some oh, so exotic deodorant.

Béatrice fitted this scenario very well: she was elegant, very slim in her spotless white jeans – very expensive ones, I felt sure – and held her head just like the models in the ads. Perhaps she had once been one, but no, that did not fit the story as I had been told it. In any case, she might have been willing to ascend the dais once, but certainly not the twenty or more times that the television models must surely have had to do. As her husband had said: *'La vie n'est pas toujours facile avec ma femme.'* No, life was not easy with her and I was beginning to see just how difficult it was, not only for him, but for me too, groping as I was between these two equally improbable but seemingly plausible characters.

She described her *cuisine équipée* which, *naturellement*, she intended to bring with her. It was in limed oak, not just the doors, of course, but the entire thing: sides, backs, shelves and all. She could not say how many units it comprised, but it held everything, this fitted kitchen of hers, and was obviously her pride and joy, after her wardrobes.

Oh yes, there had to be a space for her two washing machines – she had to have two, you know, with the horses. I must have looked puzzled, for she went on to explain that horse blankets have to be washed frequently, as indeed did her white jeans – which she wore mainly when tending the horses, and naturally would never wear a second time without washing them. And of course there was no way she was going to put her personal laundry in the same machine as the horses' stuff. So they had two machines: one for her things and the other for the horses' ... and her husband's. I do not remember how I managed to stifle a gasp of incredulity but the irrepressible burst of laughter that followed was suitably disguised as a fit of coughing. Béatrice seemed unaware of the effect she had produced, although I was not quite sure that he had not guessed my embarrassment. It seemed amazing that he could still have a sense of humour after so many years with a wife who seemed totally humourless. Perhaps it was a question of protecting his own sanity.

It was still not at all clear whether Monsieur and Madame Roger wanted my house, nor how they would propose to pay for it, and as they seemed in some hurry to leave their present place, I could not understand why these issues were not being discussed. And, of course, I was not yet certain that I was going to sell.

If they had been living in France for several years, then why did their car still carry Belgian numberplates? If they were the owners of this château somewhere in the Ariège, why did they not sell it in order to buy my house, if that was what they wanted? Monsieur Roger had mentioned that he had, of course, been known in the Resistance by another name, and had further confused the Germans by inverting his first and his family name as and when it suited him. I have to admit that I never did see a reference to him under either in any book about the Resistance in Belgium. Many strange things happened at that time, I know, but it all seemed slightly odd when you thought about it.

For several days they visited the house as often as possible, and if I happened to be out, would walk everywhere they could around the house and garden, often bringing a picnic lunch – a simple sandwich of the English variety – and an apple or peach. I remember coming home from somewhere one afternoon, and finding them sitting talking together under the great walnut tree. Why a pair of pants of hers was drying on a branch of one of the cherry trees I never could be sure, but it struck me then that her evident obsession with cleanliness and spotless white clothes could have been the result of feeling defiled by her experiences at the hands of the Gestapo. On the other hand, I have known several children grow up obsessed with cleanliness and endless handwashing, so who was to know? However it was, I suddenly felt a trespasser in my own garden, stumbling on something not meant for my eyes.

She had to return to her horses again, so he drove her back to their mountain stronghold and on his return two days later rang to tell me he had had a brilliant idea and would I come and discuss it with him.

Once again I found myself immersed in his problems, but could see no way of escape. And although I could not help feeling from time to time that the whole set-up seemed odd, I found it hard to pin-point any real inconsistencies. And when someone so plausible and charming appeals for help, what can one do but give it? So I listened as he told me that their house was not in fact owned by them, but was rented from their local Commune, who now wanted it back, and were in fact harassing them to get out, all of which had greatly upset his wife, and already caused several skirmishes, as the *Maire* and village councillors had attempted, through the *huissier*, the local bailiff, to serve an eviction order on them. Fortunately the shot fired by his wife had not reached its mark.

So they were serious about buying my house, provided I agreed to his plan for payment. He could not, he said, risk dilapidating his fortune, which was in dollars, for fear that when he died his wife might not be able to manage. And he considered it likely, in view of the fact that he was so much older than her, that he would die before her, as he was, he reminded me, over seventy-five. She was only sixty, he added, and should have some more years before her, but, as I no doubt now appreciated, she needed all the security he could give her.

Then there was the question of what happened to his possessions after her death. The only thing he could not stand was the idea that her sister should inherit them, which, in accordance with Belgian law, she undoubtedly would unless he arranged things differently. So what about making me his residuary legatee, so that, after his wife's death, the house would revert to me, along with whatever remained of his fortune for good measure?

I don't know whether he really thought I would accept such an arrangement, fraught as it obviously was with snags of every kind, but he tried very hard to persuade me that it was the ideal solution. No doubt for him. Possibly for her. But certainly not for me. I needed money, not promises. If I was going to leave my beloved house, it could only be to sell it, and I did not want it back on my hands ten or twenty years later. In any case, she could well survive me, and what would have been her sister's attitude to this 'universal legatee' – a complete stranger to her, an utter impostor, this cuckoo's egg in their cosy family nest?

My reply left out the cuckoo bit. All I had to do was to remind him of what I had said when we had first met: that I needed the money from the sale of the house. Real money. Money now. I was sorry. I really was.

* * *

He was a resilient man. Mind you, the life he had been forced to lead had really stretched him, but nevertheless I could not help admiring his cheerful acceptance of my verdict: that his brilliant notion was a non-starter as far as I was concerned.

So he returned to the Ariège to fetch his wife, the three horses, the fitted kitchen, innumerable wardrobes and other moveables, including a small battered *fourgonette*, no doubt one of the horses' accoutrements, leaving behind the deep red velvet draperies and the tiled luxury bathrooms that I would never now be able to compare with the television ads. He placed the horses in temporary 'accommodation', not far from my house, and the remainder he put in store, retaining his wife with him in the hotel while they began to scour the area for an isolated house to rent, unless of course I relented and let them have mine.

The two of them continued their daily walks down to my house, picnicking in the orchard if I was not there, and no doubt continuing to use the fruit trees as washing lines. The hotel let it be known that, odd as they might be, their weekly bills were paid with impeccable punctuality in spite of their considerable size. Madame did from time to time create scenes in the dining-room, for she could not, she often said, eat anything that figured on any of the six excellent menus, but had to have some delicate morsel of her own choice cooked specially for her, a luxury that inevitably had to be paid for, but if he was prepared to pay for it, so what?

That Madame should be quirky about her food, that was understandable, so they thought in the hotel, for what true Frenchman (and this courtesy title was extended in this instance to the Belgians, even to Belgian women), what true Frenchman did not care passionately about his food? But that she should ill-treat him, that was unforgivable. He was beyond reproach. Quite delightful.

'She does, you know!' The voice dropped to a mere whisper while a pair of radar eyes scanned the area within earshot to make sure we were not overheard.

'You know that tiny *fourgonette* of theirs, the battered old van they leave in the car-park? Well, I've seen him climb out of that at five in the morning, when she's locked him out of their room in a fit of pique about something or other. Can you imagine having to sleep in a thing like that? He looks sprightly enough, but you know he's pushing seventy-six! It's not right, is it? You can't even stretch out full length in the back of those, can you?'

The manageress, plump, pretty and charming, who most certainly would never have dreamt of locking her husband out of his rightful place beside her in their cosy double bed, threw up her hands and raised her eyes in indignation, then, after another quick scan, went on: 'When I realized what was going on, I thought "to hell with discretion" and handed him the keys of a room that is hardly ever occupied, so that at least he has a bed to sleep in. After all, you can't sit there and watch such things going on without wanting to help where possible, can you?'

How well I understood her. One simply had to do what one could to make life tolerable for this selfless man who, without a word of complaint, had carried his cross daily, hourly, for over forty years, and managed most of the time to make it look as if he enjoyed it. I felt ashamed at having ever questioned his authenticity, at having thought I might, just might, have been facing a confidence trickster.

They remained in the hotel for nearly six months, except on Tuesdays, when Madame, unable to bear the sounds and smells of the weekly market, would take her husband off to an extremely expensive place in the middle of nowhere, and occupy the best room for which they paid a permanent retainer, until Wednesday brought peace back to the small town. They paid all their bills, looked after their horses, and continued to seek unfurnished lodgings with grounds.

Eventually he found a large, old-fashioned house to rent on the far edge of a village not far from La Motte. It had three hectares of land – plenty for the horses – and a barn where they could be stabled. The plumbing and electrics dated from around 1920 – no tiled dais in the bathroom here, if indeed there was a bathroom – and it had been unoccupied since the owners, three elderly sisters, all born there towards the end of the last century, had died within a few months of each other some ten years back.

Béatrice had visions of grandiose proportions for the house: everything had to be changed. I could only see a dreadful little kitchen with five doors and an ugly old-fashioned open fireplace, and wondered whether even her solid oak cabinets could redeem the irredeemable. There was a *cabinet de toilette* off one of the upstairs rooms, with a bidet and a wash basin, and the main bedroom actually had a bathroom with a cast-iron bath on claw-footed legs, a bidet and a wash-basin. No tiles. Not one. As the only taps were over the basin and bidet, and offered only cold water, one had to surmise that hot water had been carried upstairs in a bucket whenever anyone actually wanted to take a bath. As for the only loo, it appeared to be off the kitchen, and I did not dare investigate any further.

When the Rogers had more or less settled in, I was invited to see the transformations and have a drink.

'My wife likes you,' Monsieur Roger told me in confidential tones. 'She doesn't get on with most people, but she seems to trust you. So do come and have a drink with us. It's so rare for her to want to. I can never be sure with her what will please her and what she will take against. At the moment she's got it in for the people up the road because of their coffee.'

'Their coffee?' I asked, puzzled.

'Yes, she is very sensitive to smells, and the smell of other people's coffee seems to upset her out of all proportion. She locks herself into the house and closes every window and door at the times they make coffee. She says the smell is nauseating and makes her ill. Funny, because she drinks the stuff herself.'

It was a strange evening, something hovering between the urbane and the surreal. Of course I had to do a tour of the house. The fitted kitchen did not fit, as I had feared, and the glorious rosewood wardrobes looked rather pathetically 1930-ish in the dreary, high-ceilinged bedroom she had chosen as her domain. Not at all as I had imagined them, but she obviously saw things differently. I wondered about those magnificent bathrooms in the previous house.

We drank an excellent white wine, more of it than I would have chosen, but with her there was no choice. 'I would be insulted if you refused another glass. Never heard of such nonsense; we're only on the third bottle and the evening is before us. Henri, pour her some more while I make some sandwiches!'

When she left the room I whispered something about really needing to get home. I had already been there too long, I feared.

'No, *please* don't go. You've no idea how much pleasure your visit is giving her. She would be devastated if you were to go now. Stay on for what she calls a sandwich. I would so much appreciate it.'

So I stayed, and drank as little more as I decently could, and ate her excellent sandwiches: large roughly-cut rounds of bread and butter smothered in smoked salmon. Nothing else, but quite delicious. It was an extraordinary evening, fraught with hazards like an ill-mapped coastline, but I somehow managed to avoid the most dangerous shoals. I felt like Alice talking to the Red Queen, but at least my hostess never actually said 'Off with her head!'

They stayed on in that house for about three years, then suddenly I did not see them around any more. Perhaps the smell of the neighbour's coffee became unbearable. I shall probably never know.

I did decide to sell my house in the end, since there were indeed problems with Fernando, as I had feared there might be. But that is another story. And then, quite unexpectedly, I met a wonderful man and we decided to marry. But we did not go far away, and I kept in touch with most of my old friends.

And for a long time after I had sold 'La Maison Jeanblanc' I would hear that a mysterious couple were seen quite frequently walking along the kilometre of track towards the old house, turning back just before reaching the house itself. The man looked very English and the woman always wore white, but the new owners never once managed to get close enough to them to see their faces.